ULTIMATE SOUP MAKER

An Hachette UK Company
www.hachette.co.uk

First published in Great Britain in 2020 by Hamlyn, an imprint of
Octopus Publishing Group Ltd
Carmelite House
50 Victoria Embankment
London EC4Y 0DZ
www.octopusbooks.co.uk
www.octopusbooksusa.com

Distributed in the US by
Hachette Book Group
1290 Avenue of the Americas
4th and 5th Floors
New York, NY 10104

Distributed in Canada by
Canadian Manda Group
664 Annette St.
Toronto, Ontario, Canada M6S 2C8

Some of the recipes in this book may have previously
appeared in other books by Hamlyn.

ISBN 978-0-600-63641-0

A CIP catalogue record for this book is available from the
British Library.

Printed and bound in China

10 9 8 7 6 5

FSC
www.fsc.org
MIX
Paper from
responsible sources
FSC® C008047

Standard level spoon measurements are used in all recipes.
1 tablespoon = one 15 ml spoon
1 teaspoon = one 5 ml spoon

Both imperial and metric measurements have been given
in all recipes. Use one set of measurements only and not a
mixture of both.

hamlyn

ULTIMATE SOUP MAKER

JOY SKIPPER

MORE THAN 100 SIMPLE NUTRITIOUS RECIPES

CONTENTS

INTRODUCTION

From light lunches to something more substantial – soups can be healthy, comforting, hearty and nourishing, as well as easy to incorporate into your daily diet. Homemade soup tastes delicious, is inexpensive to prepare and can make a sustaining, healthy meal for the whole family. Cooking from scratch ensures you know exactly what you are eating, without any of the preservatives or ingredients often listed on packets or tins of processed foods. Now preparing soup at home is easier than ever before.

Using a soup maker allows you to cook with fresh ingredients, reduce waste and save time in the kitchen. Not only are soup makers affordable but using leftovers to create a tasty soup is an efficient way of saving money and avoiding waste. It's also easy to cook large quantities and freeze portions when you have an abundance of ingredients (when the allotment is over-producing or to use up leftovers in the refrigerator, for example). Most soups are easy to freeze in single portions, so when you need a quick meal it's simply a case of microwaving a portion from the freezer.

A soup maker is the equivalent of one-pot cooking – add whatever roughly diced ingredients you have to spare, whether fresh, leftover from your refrigerator or garden surplus, add herbs, spices and stock and in as little as 20–30 minutes you have delicious homemade soup. After a quick rinse the soup maker is ready to go again.

WHAT TO LOOK FOR IN A SOUP MAKER

There are lots of affordable soup makers available on the market and each one will be accompanied by a manual, do take time to examine your particular model and familiarize yourself with the settings, as these tend to vary slightly between brands. If you are planning to buy one then there are a number of things to consider, as some have more advanced features than others:

Sauté function – heats the cooking jug so you can sauté some of the base ingredients, such as bacon, onions, celery, peppers and spices, before the rest of the ingredients are added. Sautéing ingredients in the same jug as the soup is cooked improves the taste, as all of the flavour is retained during the cooking process.

Smooth setting – perfect for soup recipes that require a smooth consistency, such as Spiced Parsnip and Red Lentil (page 55), Savoy Cabbage and Parmesan (page 111) and Smoky Carrot and Sweet Potato (page 59). The program ensures the ingredients are blended to a smooth, lump-free consistency and gently cooked at the right temperature.

Chunky setting – good for more rustic soups such as Spring Minestrone (page 91), Russian Borsch (page 105) and Tomato, Lentil and Aubergine (page 60), requiring a chunkier consistency. The program allows the ingredients to be heated for longer to ensure the chunky ingredients are fully cooked.

Blender function – this allows blending after the soup is made, and further ingredients can also be added to the cooked soup before it is blended. This setting does not heat the soup.

Juicer – some soup makers can also be used as a juicer for making smoothies or milkshakes from fresh ingredients. This setting does not heat the ingredients.

USING YOUR SOUP MAKER

There are some factors to take into consideration when using your soup maker:

The capacity of the soup maker: This will vary depending on the brand of soup maker you have, so do check the minimum and maximum levels and ensure you stick to them when adding ingredients. If you need to add a little less liquid you may have a thicker consistency soup that can be loosened with extra stock, cream or other liquid when the soup is cooked and served.

Sauté function in soup makers: In most cases this can only be used with the lid removed from the jug and for no longer than 10 minutes. Sautéing is perfect for onions, celery, peppers, carrots or bacon lardons where they need to be softened or browned. To achieve the best results, cut vegetables into small cubes before frying them in the soup maker, especially if making a smooth soup. Aside from bacon and small amounts of mince (up to 100 g/3½ oz), meat cannot be cooked using the sauté function or in the soup maker without being pre-cooked first, either by roasting, grilling or frying. If your soup maker does not have a sauté function it is best to prepare ingredients in a heavy-based pan before transferring to your soup maker.

Achieving the desired consistency: For chunky soup there is no blending required and it is advised that the vegetables are cut into small bite-sized pieces at the start of the Chunky program. If the soup is a little too chunky after cooking, your soup maker may have a blender function (see previous page) that you can use to achieve the desired consistency.

Can ingredients be added during cooking?
This will depend on the soup maker you are using, but some models allow the lid to be removed during the cooking program (but not while the machine is blending) so ingredients that need less cooking time can be added. Using a timer when your soup maker is cooking is very useful to understand what stage it is at, so you can add ingredients before it starts to blend, for example. Beware attempting to remove the lid during blending – it will cause a lot of mess!

How long will the soup take to cook?
Typically most programs take between 20–30 minutes, depending on your machine and the program you are using. This is exclusive of time spent sautéing using models which permit this feature.

The recipes in this book were tested with a soup maker with a minimum capacity of 1.3 litres (2¼ pints) and a maximum of 1.6 litres (2¾ pints). The soup maker also featured a sauté function which allowed the cooking process to be paused and the lid removed so that further ingredients can be added.

It is worth noting that you should not sauté in a soup maker for longer than 10 minutes for risk of the ingredients getting burnt.

If your soup maker does not have a sauté function, this step can be done in a saucepan, transferring the ingredients to the soup maker after sautéing and before cooking on the Smooth or Chunky setting.

For many soup makers the average cooking time for Smooth is 20 minutes whereas for Chunky the cycle takes 30 minutes.

You may need to adjust the amount of liquid specified for the recipes in this book depending on the minimum and maximum levels set on your soup maker. This may change the consistency of the soup; if it is too thick at the end of the cooking program, stirring in a little boiling water or warmed milk may help to loosen it.

SKINNY

COURGETTE AND DILL

SERVES 4

2 tablespoons sunflower or light olive oil

1 large onion, diced

2 garlic cloves, crushed

500 g (1 lb) courgettes, thinly sliced

800 ml (1½ pints) vegetable or chicken stock

1–2 tablespoons finely chopped dill, plus extra fronds to garnish

salt and pepper

50 ml (2 fl oz) single cream, to serve

○ Illustrated on page 10.

○ Heat the oil in the soup maker using the sauté function. Add the onion and garlic and sauté for 5 minutes until softened, but not browned, stirring frequently with a wooden spatula.

○ Add the courgettes, stock and dill, then cook on the Smooth setting.

○ Season the soup to taste, then pour into warm bowls. Swirl through the cream and serve garnished with the dill fronds.

SERVES 4-6

3 tablespoons extra virgin olive oil, plus extra to serve

1 onion, diced

2 garlic cloves, finely chopped

2 teaspoons finely chopped thyme

250 g (8 oz) potatoes, peeled and diced

500 g (1 lb) frozen or fresh shelled peas

1 litre (1¾ pints) vegetable stock

100 g (3½ oz) rocket leaves, roughly chopped

juice of 1 lemon

salt and pepper

PEA, POTATO AND ROCKET

○ Heat the oil in the soup maker using the sauté function. Add the onion, garlic and thyme and sauté for 5 minutes until the onion is softened, stirring frequently with a wooden spatula. Add the potatoes and cook for another 5 minutes, stirring frequently.

○ Stir in the peas and stock, then cook on the Smooth setting for 10 minutes. Add the rocket and lemon juice and continue to cook on Smooth.

○ Season the soup to taste, then serve in warm bowls, drizzled with a little extra olive oil.

SERVES 4–6

25 g (1 oz) butter or margarine

½ tablespoon olive oil

1 onion, diced

2 carrots, diced

500 g (1 lb) kale, thick stems removed and leaves finely shredded, plus 2 leaves, thinly shredded

1 litre (1¾ pints) vegetable stock

1 tablespoon lemon juice

200 g (7 oz) potatoes, peeled and diced

pinch of grated nutmeg

salt and pepper

FOR THE GARLIC CROUTONS

4 tablespoons olive oil

3 garlic cloves, sliced

2–4 slices of white or brown bread, crusts removed, cut into 1 cm (½ inch) cubes

KALE WITH GARLIC CROUTONS

○ Heat the butter or margarine and oil in the soup maker using the sauté function. Add the onion and sauté for 5 minutes until softened, stirring frequently with a wooden spatula. Add the carrots and kale and cook for another 2–3 minutes, stirring frequently.

○ Add the stock, lemon juice, potatoes and nutmeg, then cook on the Smooth setting.

○ Meanwhile, make the croutons. Heat the oil in a frying pan, add the garlic and cook over a medium heat for 1 minute. Add the bread cubes and fry until evenly golden brown, turning frequently. Remove with a slotted spoon and drain on kitchen paper.

○ Discard the garlic from the frying pan, then add the 2 shredded kale leaves and fry until crispy, stirring constantly.

○ Season the soup to taste, then serve in warm bowls, sprinkled with the garlic croutons and crispy kale.

SERVES 4

2 tablespoons olive oil, plus extra to serve

3 fat spring onions, trimmed and thinly sliced

250 g (8 oz) fennel bulb, trimmed, cored and thinly sliced

1 potato, peeled and diced

finely grated zest and juice of 1 lemon

1.5 litres (2½ pints) vegetable stock

salt and pepper

toasted crusty bread, to serve (optional)

FOR THE GREMOLATA

1 small garlic clove, finely chopped

grated zest of 1 lemon

4 tablespoons chopped parsley

16 black olives, pitted and chopped

FENNEL AND LEMON

○ Heat the oil in the soup maker using the sauté function. Add the spring onions and sauté for 5 minutes, stirring frequently with a wooden spatula. Add the fennel, potato and lemon zest and cook for another 5 minutes until the fennel begins to soften, stirring frequently.

○ Pour in the stock, then cook on the Smooth setting.

○ Meanwhile, make the gremolata. Mix together all the ingredients in a small bowl, then cover and chill.

○ Season the soup with salt, pepper and lemon juice to taste.

○ Pour into warm bowls, drizzle with olive oil and sprinkle with the gremolata. Serve with toasted crusty bread, if liked.

SERVES 4

1 tablespoon olive oil

1 leek, trimmed, cleaned and thinly sliced

1 large potato, peeled and diced

450 g (14½ oz) mixed summer vegetables, such as peas, asparagus, broad beans and diced courgettes

2 tablespoons chopped mint

900 ml (1½ pints) vegetable stock

2 tablespoons low-fat crème fraîche

salt and pepper

SUMMER VEGETABLE

○ Heat the oil in the soup maker using the sauté function. Add the leek and sauté for 3–4 minutes until softened, stirring frequently with a wooden spatula.

○ Add the potato, summer vegetables, mint and stock, then cook on the Smooth setting.

○ Stir the crème fraîche into the soup, then season to taste. Serve in warm bowls.

1 tablespoon olive oil

1 tablespoon butter

1 Bramley apple, peeled, cored and diced

1 dessert apple, peeled, cored and diced

625 g (1¼ lb) cooked beetroot, roughly diced

2 teaspoons caraway seeds

1 teaspoon thyme leaves

1.2 litres (2 pints) vegetable stock

salt and pepper

crème fraîche, to serve

chopped dill, to garnish

BEETROOT AND APPLE

○ Heat the oil and butter in the soup maker using the sauté function. Add the apples and sauté for 2–3 minutes, stirring frequently with a wooden spatula. Add the beetroot, caraway seeds and thyme and cook for another 2–3 minutes, stirring frequently.

○ Pour in the stock, then cook on the Smooth setting.

○ Season the soup to taste, then pour into warm bowls. Swirl through the crème fraîche and serve garnished with chopped dill and freshly ground black pepper.

SPICED COCONUT SQUASH

SERVES 4

2 tablespoons olive oil

1 onion, diced

2 teaspoons peeled and diced fresh root ginger

1 teaspoon ground coriander

½ lemon grass stalk, diced

1 strip of orange rind

800 g (1½ lb) butternut squash, peeled, deseeded and diced

800 ml (1⅓ pints) vegetable stock

125 ml (4 fl oz) coconut milk

salt and pepper

TO GARNISH

1 red chilli, chopped

fresh coriander leaves, chopped

○ Heat the oil in the soup maker using the sauté function. Add the onion and sauté for 5 minutes until softened, stirring frequently with a wooden spatula.

○ Add the ginger, ground coriander, lemon grass, orange rind and squash. Pour in the stock and coconut milk, then cook on the Smooth setting.

○ Season the soup to taste, then serve in warm bowls, sprinkled with the chopped chilli and coriander.

SERVES 4

3 green apples

1–2 tablespoons olive oil

20 g (¾ oz) butter

1 onion, diced

25 g (1 oz) fresh root ginger, peeled and finely chopped

2 teaspoons fennel seeds

1 teaspoon coriander seeds

1 teaspoon cumin seeds

1 teaspoon sugar

1 small butternut squash, about 900 g (2 lb), peeled, deseeded and diced

1 litre (1¾ pints) chicken stock

150 ml (¼ pint) double cream

salt and pepper

chilli oil, to serve

APPLE AND BUTTERNUT SQUASH WITH CHILLI OIL

○ Preheat the oven to 150°C (300°F), Gas Mark 2. Core and very thinly slice 1 of the apples horizontally to form thin discs. Place on a wire rack set over a baking sheet and bake for 20–25 minutes. Peel, core and dice the remaining apples.

○ Meanwhile, heat the oil and butter in the soup maker using the sauté function. Add the onion, ginger, spices and sugar and sauté for 1–2 minutes, stirring with a wooden spatula. Add the squash and cook for another 2–3 minutes, stirring to coat well.

○ Add the diced apples and stock, then cook on the Chunky setting.

○ Stir in the cream and season the soup to taste.

○ Pour into warm bowls, garnish with the baked apple slices and serve drizzled with a little chilli oil.

SERVES 4

1 tablespoon butter

1 tablespoon olive oil

8 spring onions, trimmed and thinly sliced

750 g (1½ lb) frozen peas

1 tablespoon chopped tarragon leaves, plus extra sprigs to garnish (optional)

1 romaine lettuce, finely shredded

1 litre (1¾ pints) vegetable stock

2 tablespoons single cream, plus extra to serve

salt and pepper

LETTUCE, PEA AND TARRAGON

○ Heat the butter and oil in the soup maker using the sauté function. Add the spring onions and sauté for 3 minutes, stirring continuously with a wooden spatula. Stir in the frozen peas, chopped tarragon and lettuce and cook for another 1 minute.

○ Pour in the stock, then cook on the Smooth setting for 10 minutes. Add the cream, season to taste and continue to cook on Smooth.

○ Serve the soup in warm bowls, garnished with extra tarragon and cream, if liked.

SERVES 6

40 g (1½ oz) butter

½ tablespoon olive oil

1 onion, diced

500 g (1 lb) broccoli, cut into small florets and stems thinly sliced

40 g (1½ oz) ground almonds

900 ml (1½ pints) vegetable or chicken stock

300 ml (½ pint) milk

3 tablespoons flaked almonds

salt and pepper

6 tablespoons natural yogurt, to serve

BROCCOLI AND ALMOND

○ Heat half the butter and the oil in the soup maker using the sauté function. Add the onion and sauté for 5 minutes until softened, stirring frequently with a wooden spatula. Stir in the broccoli until coated in the butter.

○ Add the ground almonds, stock and a little salt and pepper. Cook on the Smooth setting for 10 minutes. Add the milk and continue to cook on Smooth.

○ Meanwhile, heat the remaining butter in a frying pan, add the flaked almonds and fry for a few minutes, stirring until golden.

○ Serve the soup in warm bowls, drizzled with the yogurt and sprinkled with the flaked almonds.

SERVES 6

1 tablespoon sunflower oil

1 onion, diced

4 teaspoons Thai red curry paste

1 teaspoon galangal paste

2 garlic cloves, finely chopped

1 kg (2 lb) butternut squash, peeled, deseeded and diced

250 ml (8 fl oz) coconut cream

750 ml (1¼ pints) vegetable stock

1 tablespoon soy sauce

small bunch of fresh coriander, chopped, a few sprigs reserved to garnish

salt and pepper

THAI COCONUT AND BUTTERNUT SQUASH

O Heat the oil in the soup maker using the sauté function. Add the onion and sauté for 5 minutes until softened, stirring frequently with a wooden spatula. Stir in the curry paste, galangal paste and garlic and cook for another 1 minute, stirring.

O Stir in the squash, then pour in the coconut cream, stock and soy sauce. Cook on the Smooth setting.

O Season the soup to taste, then stir in the chopped coriander. Serve in warm bowls, garnished with coriander sprigs.

PEA, LETTUCE AND LEMON WITH SESAME CROUTONS

SERVES 4

25 g (1 oz) butter

½ tablespoon olive oil

1 large onion, diced

425 g (14 oz) frozen peas

2 little gem lettuces, roughly chopped

900 ml (1½ pints) vegetable stock

grated zest and juice of ½ lemon

salt and pepper

ready-made croutons, to serve

○ Heat the butter and oil in the soup maker using the sauté function. Add the onion and cook for 5 minutes until softened, stirring frequently with a wooden spatula.

○ Add the peas, lettuces, stock and lemon zest and juice, then cook on the Smooth setting.

○ Season the soup to taste, then serve in warm bowls, sprinkled with the croutons.

GARDEN HERB

SERVES 4

50 g (2 oz) butter

½ tablespoon olive oil

1 onion, diced

1 baking potato, about 250 g (8 oz), peeled and diced

1 litre (1¾ pints) ham, chicken or vegetable stock

75 g (3 oz) mixed parsley and chives, roughly torn into pieces

salt and pepper

toasted bacon sandwiches, to serve

○ Heat the butter and oil in the soup maker using the sauté function. Add the onion and sauté for 5 minutes until softened, stirring frequently. Add the potato and cook for another 4–5 minutes, stirring frequently.

○ Add the stock and herbs, then cook on the Smooth setting.

○ Season the soup to taste, then serve in mugs with toasted bacon sandwiches (if you are feeling like something more substantial!).

SPICY AVOCADO

SERVES 4

1 tablespoon olive oil

1 onion, diced

1 fresh jalapeño chilli, deseeded and finely chopped

1 garlic clove, finely chopped

1 potato, peeled and diced

900 ml (1½ pints) vegetable stock

juice of 1 lime

150 ml (¼ pint) single cream

2 large avocados, peeled, stoned and chopped

salt and pepper

TO GARNISH

handful of coriander leaves, chopped

1 tomato, diced

○ Heat the oil in the soup maker using the sauté function. Add the onion, chilli, garlic and potato and cook for 5 minutes until softened, stirring frequently with a wooden spatula.

○ Pour in the stock, then cook on the Smooth setting for 10 minutes. Add the lime juice, double cream and avocado. Continue to cook on Smooth.

○ Season the soup to taste, then serve in warm bowls, sprinkled with the coriander leaves and tomato.

SWEETCORN AND CELERY

SERVES 6

4 corn cobs

50 g (2 oz) butter

½ tablespoon olive oil

1 onion, diced

3 celery sticks, diced

2 garlic cloves, finely chopped

1 litre (1¾ pints) chicken or vegetable stock

salt and pepper

a pinch of cayenne pepper

chilli and tomato chutney, to serve

○ Using a sharp knife, cut the kernels from the corn cobs.

○ Heat the butter and oil in the soup maker using the sauté function. Add the onion and sauté for 5 minutes until softened, stirring frequently with a wooden spatula. Add the sweetcorn kernels, celery and garlic and cook for another 3–4 minutes, stirring frequently.

○ Pour in the stock and add a pinch of cayenne pepper, then cook on the Smooth setting.

○ Season the soup with salt and cayenne pepper to taste. Serve in warm bowls, topped with spoonfuls of chilli and tomato chutney.

GINGERED CAULIFLOWER

SERVES 6

1 tablespoon sunflower oil

25 g (1 oz) butter

1 onion, diced

1 cauliflower, core discarded and florets cut into small pieces, about 500 g (1 lb) prepared weight

3.5 cm (1½ inch) piece of fresh root ginger, peeled and finely chopped

900 ml (1½ pints) vegetable or chicken stock

300 ml (½ pint) semi-skimmed milk

150 ml (¼ pint) double cream

salt and pepper

FOR THE GLAZED SEEDS

1 tablespoon sunflower oil

2 tablespoons sesame seeds

2 tablespoons sunflower seeds

2 tablespoons pumpkin seeds

1 tablespoon soy sauce

○ Heat the oil and butter in the soup maker using the sauté function. Add the onion and sauté for 5 minutes until softened but not browned, stirring frequently with a wooden spatula.

○ Stir in the cauliflower florets and ginger. Pour in the stock and milk, then cook on the Smooth setting.

○ Meanwhile, make the glazed seeds. Heat the oil in a frying pan, add the seeds and cook for 2–3 minutes, stirring until lightly browned. Add the soy sauce, then quickly cover the pan with a lid until the seeds have stopped popping. Set aside.

○ Stir half of the cream into the soup and season to taste.

○ Pour into warm bowls, drizzle over the remaining cream and sprinkle with some of the glazed seeds. Serve with the remaining seeds in a small bowl on the side.

SERVES 6

25 g (1 oz) butter

½ tablespoon olive oil

1 onion, diced

1 baking potato, about 250 g (8 oz), peeled and diced

1 cooking apple, about 250 g (8 oz), cored, peeled and diced

1 head of celery, trimmed and diced, leaves reserved for garnish

900 ml (1½ pints) chicken or vegetable stock

300 ml (½ pint) milk

salt and pepper

TO SERVE

50 g (2 oz) Stilton cheese

25 g (1 oz) walnut pieces, chopped

6 tablespoons crème fraîche

2 tablespoons chopped chives or tops of 2 spring onions, chopped

APPLE AND CELERY

○ Heat the butter and oil in the soup maker using the sauté function. Add the onion and sauté for 5 minutes until softened, stirring frequently with a wooden spatula. Stir in the potato, apple and celery and cook for another 5 minutes, stirring frequently.

○ Pour in the stock, then cook on the Smooth setting for 10 minutes. Add the milk and continue to cook on Smooth.

○ Meanwhile, mix together half the diced stilton, half the walnuts and the crème fraîche in a small bowl, then stir in the chives or spring onions and a little salt and pepper.

○ Season the soup to taste, then pour into warm bowls. Spoon on the crème fraîche mixture and serve sprinkled with the remaining cheese and nuts and a little black pepper.

SERVES 4

1 tablespoon olive oil, plus extra to serve

500 g (1 lb) leeks, trimmed, cleaned and thinly sliced

500 ml (17 fl oz) vegetable stock

60 g (2 oz) rocket leaves

125 ml (4 fl oz) crème fraîche

200 ml (7 fl oz) soya milk

salt and pepper

LEEK AND ROCKET

○ Heat the oil in the soup maker using the sauté function. Add the leeks and sauté for 4–5 minutes until softened, stirring frequently with a wooden spatula.

○ Add the stock and rocket leaves, then cook on the Smooth setting for 10 minutes. Add the crème fraîche and milk and continue to cook on Smooth.

○ Season the soup to taste, then serve in warm bowls, drizzled with a little olive oil.

SERVES 4

1 tablespoon sunflower oil

1 red onion, diced

1 celery stick, diced

1 teaspoon chopped thyme

500 g (1 lb) raw beetroot, peeled and diced

1 tablespoon red wine vinegar

1 litre (1¾ pints) vegetable stock

2 tablespoons creamed horseradish sauce

salt and pepper

chopped chives, to garnish

crusty bread, to serve

FOR THE HORSERADISH CREAM

3 tablespoons soured cream or crème fraîche

2 teaspoons creamed horseradish sauce

BEETROOT AND HORSERADISH

○ Heat the oil in the soup maker using the sauté function. Add the onion, celery and thyme and sauté for 5 minutes until softened, stirring frequently with a wooden spatula. Add the beetroot and vinegar and cook, stirring, for another 2 minutes.

○ Pour in the stock, then cook on the Smooth setting for 10 minutes. Add the horseradish sauce and continue to cook on Smooth.

○ Meanwhile, make the horseradish cream, mixing together the ingredients in a small bowl. Cover and chill.

○ Season the soup to taste, then pour into warm bowls. Spoon on the horseradish cream and garnish with chopped chives. Serve with crusty bread.

SERVES 4

50 g (2 oz) butter

2 tablespoons olive oil

1 onion, diced

2 garlic cloves, finely chopped

1 kg (2 lb) pumpkin, peeled, deseeded and diced

1 teaspoon ground coriander

½ teaspoon cayenne pepper

½ teaspoon ground cinnamon

¼ teaspoon ground allspice

1 litre (1¾ pints) vegetable stock

150 g (5 oz) frozen spinach

2 tablespoons pumpkin seeds

salt and pepper

4 teaspoons olive oil to serve

SPICED PUMPKIN AND SPINACH

○ Heat the butter and olive oil in the soup maker using the sauté function. Add the onion and garlic and sauté for 4–5 minutes until softened, stirring frequently with a wooden spatula. Add the pumpkin and cook, stirring, for another 3–4 minutes. Add the spices and stir well to coat the pumpkin.

○ Pour in the stock and stir in the spinach, then cook on the Smooth setting.

○ Meanwhile, heat a nonstick frying pan over a medium-low heat and dry-fry the pumpkin seeds for 2–3 minutes until slightly golden and toasted, stirring frequently. Set aside.

○ Season the soup to taste, then serve in warm bowls, sprinkled with the toasted pumpkin seeds and drizzled with oil.

SUPER SIMPLE

ROASTED PUMPKIN WITH CRISPY BACON

SERVES 4

1 kg (2 lb) pumpkin, peeled, deseeded and cut into chunks

2 tablespoons olive oil

1 large onion, diced

2 garlic cloves, crushed

½ teaspoon smoked paprika

1.2 litres (2 pints) chicken stock

4 rindless streaky bacon rashers

salt and pepper

○ Ilustrated on page 32.

○ Preheat the oven to 200°C (400°F), Gas Mark 6. Place the pumpkin in a roasting tray and drizzle with 1 tablespoon of the olive oil. Roast for 25 minutes until tender, tossing occasionally.

○ Heat the remaining oil in the soup maker using the sauté function. Add the onion and sauté for 4–5 minutes until softened, stirring frequently with a wooden spatula. Add the garlic and paprika and cook, stirring, for another 1 minute.

○ Add the roasted pumpkin to the soup maker, then pour in the stock and cook on the Smooth setting.

○ Meanwhile, place the bacon rashers on a foil-lined grill pan and cook under a preheated grill for 5–6 minutes until crispy and golden, turning occasionally. Chop or crumble the grilled bacon into small pieces. Drain on kitchen paper.

○ Season the soup to taste, then serve in warm bowls, sprinkled with the bacon bits.

SERVES 6

2 tablespoons olive oil

375 g (12 oz) leeks, trimmed, cleaned and thinly sliced

375 g (12 oz) fresh shelled or frozen peas

900 ml (1½ pints) vegetable or chicken stock

small bunch of mint, finely chopped, plus extra leaves to garnish (optional)

150 g (5 oz) mascarpone cheese

grated zest of 1 small lemon

salt and pepper

lemon rind curls, to garnish (optional)

CREAM OF LEEK AND PEA

○ Heat the oil in the soup maker using the sauté function. Add the leeks and sauté for 5 minutes until softened but not browned, stirring occasionally with a wooden spatula. Add the peas and cook, stirring, for another 1–2 minutes.

○ Pour in the stock, add a little salt and pepper and then cook on the Chunky setting.

○ Turn the soup maker off and on again to activate the blender function. Add the mint and pulse 3 or 4 times to blend a little, while still retaining some chunks.

○ Mix the mascarpone with half of the lemon zest, reserving the rest for garnish. Spoon half the mixture into the soup and stir until the mascarpone has melted. Season to taste.

○ Pour the soup into bowls and top with spoonfuls of the remaining mascarpone and a sprinkling of the remaining lemon zest. Serve garnished with mint leaves and lemon rind curls, if liked.

SERVES 4

2 tablespoons olive oil

1 onion, diced

2 red peppers, cored, deseeded and diced

750 g (1½ lb) tomatoes, roughly diced

1 garlic clove, finely chopped

900 ml (1½ pints) vegetable stock

1 tablespoon tomato purée

2 teaspoons caster sugar

1 tablespoon balsamic vinegar,

salt and pepper

ready-made pesto, to serve

TOMATO AND RED PEPPER

O Heat the oil in the soup maker using the sauté function. Add the onion and sauté for 5 minutes until softened, stirring frequently with a wooden spatula. Add the red peppers and tomatoes and cook, stirring, for another 1–2 minutes.

O Add the stock, tomato purée, sugar and vinegar, then cook on the Smooth setting.

O Season the soup to taste, then serve in warm bowls, with a swirl of pesto to finish.

SERVES 4

1 kg (2 lb) butternut squash, peeled, deseeded and chopped

1½ tablespoons olive oil

1 teaspoon dried chilli flakes

2 teaspoons cumin seeds

2 tablespoons pumpkin seeds

1 onion, diced

1 garlic clove, chopped

900 ml (1½ pints) vegetable stock

salt and pepper

2 tablespoons natural yogurt, to serve

BUTTERNUT AND CUMIN

○ Preheat the oven to 200°C (400°F), Gas Mark 6. Place the squash in a roasting tray, drizzle with 1 tablespoon of the oil and sprinkle with the chilli flakes and cumin seeds. Roast for 20–25 minutes until tender, tossing occasionally.

○ Meanwhile, heat a nonstick frying pan over a medium-low heat and dry-fry the pumpkin seeds for 2–3 minutes until slightly golden and toasted, stirring frequently. Set aside.

○ Heat the remaining oil using the sauté function. Add the onion and garlic and sauté for 3–4 minutes until beginning to soften, stirring frequently with a wooden spatula.

○ Add the roasted squash and pour in the stock, then cook on the Smooth setting.

○ Season the soup to taste, then pour into warm bowls. Serve topped with the yogurt and the toasted pumpkin seeds.

PUMPKIN WITH OLIVE SALSA

SERVES 6

4 tablespoons olive oil

1 large onion, diced

2 garlic cloves, crushed

½ tablespoon finely chopped sage

875 g (1¾ lb) pumpkin, peeled, deseeded and cubed

400 g (13 oz) can cannellini or haricot beans, rinsed and drained

1 litre (1¾ pints) vegetable stock

salt and pepper

FOR THE OLIVE SALSA

100 g (3½ oz) pitted black olives, finely diced

3 tablespoons extra virgin olive oil

grated zest of 1 lemon

2 tablespoons chopped parsley

○ Heat the olive oil in the soup maker using the sauté function. Add the onion, garlic and sage and sauté for 5 minutes until softened, stirring frequently with a wooden spatula.

○ Add the pumpkin and beans and stir well, then add the stock and a little salt and pepper. Cook on the Smooth setting.

○ Meanwhile, make the olive salsa by mixing together all the ingredients in a bowl.

○ Serve the soup in warm bowls with a spoonful of olive salsa sprinkled over the top of each.

SERVES 4

1 tablespoon sunflower oil

1 large onion, diced

625 g (1¼ lb) carrots, diced

1½ teaspoons cumin seeds, roughly crushed

1 teaspoon ground turmeric

50 g (2 oz) long-grain rice

1 litre (1¾ pints) vegetable stock

salt and pepper

TO SERVE

150 g (5 oz) natural yogurt

mango chutney

a few poppadums

CARROT AND CUMIN

○ Heat the oil in the soup maker using the sauté function. Add the onion and sauté for 4–5 minutes until softened, stirring frequently with a wooden spatula. Stir in the carrots, cumin seeds and turmeric and cook, stirring, for another 2–3 minutes to release the cumin flavour and brown the onion.

○ Stir in the rice and stock, then cook on the Smooth setting.

○ Season the soup to taste, then pour into warm bowls. Top with the yogurt and a little mango chutney and serve with poppadums.

SERVES 4

15 g (½ oz) butter

1 tablespoon olive oil

500 g (1 lb) potatoes, peeled and diced

2 leeks, trimmed, cleaned and thinly sliced

900 ml (1½ pints) vegetable stock

300 g (10 oz) frozen peas

salt and pepper

FOR THE PESTO CHEESY TOASTS

4 slices of French baguette

2 tablespoons pesto

125 g (4 oz) Gruyère cheese, grated

PEA, LEEK AND POTATO WITH PESTO CHEESY TOASTS

○ Heat the butter and oil in the soup maker using the sauté function. Add the potatoes and leeks and sauté for 5 minutes until softened, stirring frequently with a wooden spatula.

○ Pour in the stock, then cook on the Smooth setting for 10 minutes. Add the peas and continue to cook on Smooth.

○ Meanwhile, toast the baguette slices on one side under a preheated grill. Turn the slices over, then spread with half the pesto and top with the cheese. Grill until melted.

○ Season the soup to taste, then pour into warm bowls. Swirl through the remaining pesto and serve with the toasts.

SERVES 4

3 tablespoons sunflower oil

1 large onion, diced

2 garlic cloves, crushed

2.5 cm (1 inch) piece of fresh root ginger, peeled and grated

1 red chilli, deseeded and diced, plus extra to garnish (optional)

1 tablespoon medium curry powder

250 g (8 oz) dried red lentils

1.3 litres (2¼ pints) vegetable stock

200 g (7 oz) canned chopped tomatoes

100 g (3½ oz) baby spinach leaves

25 g (1 oz) coriander leaves, chopped, plus extra to garnish

100 ml (3½ fl oz) coconut cream

salt and pepper

4 tablespoons natural yogurt, to serve

SPINACH AND RED LENTIL

○ Heat the oil in the soup maker using the sauté function. Add the onion and sauté for 5–6 minutes until softened, stirring frequently with a wooden spatula. Add the garlic, ginger and chilli and cook for another minute. Stir in the curry powder.

○ Add the lentils and pour in the stock, then cook on the Smooth setting for 8 minutes. Add the tomatoes, spinach, coriander, coconut cream and seasoning and continue to cook on Smooth.

○ Pour the soup into warm bowls and top with the yogurt. Serve sprinkled with the coriander leaves, freshly ground black pepper and finely chopped red chilli, if liked.

SERVES 4

4 tablespoons olive oil

800 g (1½ lb) ripe tomatoes, roughly diced

1 large red onion, diced

2 garlic cloves, crushed

800 ml (1⅓ pints) vegetable stock

2 tablespoons tomato purée

1 teaspoon caster sugar

1 teaspoon oregano leaves, plus extra leaves to garnish

1 tablespoon shredded basil leaves

4 tablespoons grated Parmesan cheese

salt and pepper

FOR THE CIABATTA CROUTONS

2 ciabatta rolls, torn into pieces

2 tablespoons olive oil

MEDITERRANEAN TOMATO WITH CIABATTA CROUTONS

○ Heat 2 tablespoons of the oil in the soup maker using the sauté function. Add the tomatoes, onion and garlic and sauté for 3–4 minutes until softened, stirring frequently with a wooden spatula.

○ Stir in the stock, tomato purée, sugar, oregano and shredded basil, then cook on the Smooth setting.

○ Meanwhile, make the croutons. Place the ciabatta pieces on a baking sheet and drizzle over the oil. Toast under a preheated medium grill for a few minutes, turning occasionally, until crisp and golden.

○ Stir half the Parmesan into the soup and season to taste.

○ Pour the soup into warm bowls, drizzle with the remaining oil and top with some of the ciabatta croutons. Sprinkle with the remaining Parmesan and a few oregano leaves. Serve with the remaining croutons.

SERVES 6

2 tablespoons sunflower oil

1 large onion, diced

4 garlic cloves, finely chopped

2 red peppers, cored, deseeded and diced

2 red chillies, deseeded and finely chopped

750 ml (1¼ pints) vegetable stock

750 ml (1¼ pints) tomato juice or passata

2 tablespoons sweet chilli sauce

400 g (13 oz) can red kidney beans, rinsed and drained

2 tablespoons finely chopped fresh coriander

salt and pepper

TO SERVE

75 ml (3 fl oz) soured cream

rind of 1 lime, cut into strips (optional)

tortilla chips

CHILLI BEAN AND RED PEPPER

○ Heat the oil in the soup maker using the sauté function. Add the onion and garlic and sauté for 5 minutes until softened, stirring frequently with a wooden spatula. Add the red peppers and chillies and cook for another 2–3 minutes, stirring frequently.

○ Stir in the stock, tomato juice or passata, chilli sauce, beans and coriander, then cook on the Smooth setting.

○ Season the soup to taste, then pour into warm bowls. Swirl through the soured cream and garnish with the lime strips, if liked. Serve with tortilla chips.

SERVES 4

25 g (1 oz) butter

1 tablespoon sunflower oil

1 onion, diced

2 garlic cloves, crushed

2.5 cm (1 inch) piece of fresh root ginger, peeled and diced

1 tablespoon medium curry powder

1 teaspoon cumin seeds

750 g (1½ lb) parsnips, diced

1 litre (1¾ pints) vegetable stock

salt and pepper

2 tablespoons chopped coriander leaves, to garnish

TO SERVE

natural yogurt

naan bread

CURRIED PARSNIP

○ Heat the butter and oil in the soup maker using the sauté function. Add the onion, garlic and ginger and sauté for 4–5 minutes until softened, stirring frequently with a wooden spatula. Stir in the curry powder and cumin seeds and cook, stirring, for another 2 minutes. Add the parsnips, stirring well to coat in the spice mixture.

○ Pour in the stock, then cook on the Smooth setting.

○ Season the soup to taste, then pour into cups. Top with dollops of yogurt, garnish with the coriander and serve with warmed naan bread.

MEXICAN BEAN

SERVES 4

2 tablespoons vegetable oil

1 large onion, diced

1 red pepper, cored, deseeded and diced

2 garlic cloves, finely chopped

30 g (1 oz) sachet Mexican fajita, taco or chilli con carne spice mix

400 g (13 oz) can kidney beans, rinsed and drained

400 g (13 oz) can black beans, rinsed and drained

400 g (13 oz) can chopped tomatoes

900 ml (1½ pints) vegetable or beef stock

TO SERVE

4 tablespoons soured cream

25 g (1 oz) tortilla chips (optional)

○ Heat the oil in the soup maker using the sauté function. Add the onion and red pepper and sauté for 5 minutes until softened, stirring frequently with a wooden spatula. Add the garlic and spice mix and cook, stirring, for another 1–2 minutes.

○ Add the beans, chopped tomatoes and stock and stir well, then cook on the Chunky setting.

○ If your model requires, turn the soup maker off and on again to activate the blender function. Pulse a few times to give the soup a thicker consistency, while still retaining some whole beans.

○ Serve the soup in warm bowls, drizzled with the soured cream and topped with the tortilla chips, if liked.

CREAM OF SWEETCORN

SERVES 4–6

40 g (1½ oz) butter

1 tablespoon olive oil

1 onion, diced

2 potatoes, peeled and diced

25 g (1 oz) plain flour

900 ml (1½ pints) milk

2 x 325 g (11 oz) cans sweetcorn, drained

6 tablespoons double cream

salt and pepper

crumbled crispy bacon (see page 34), to garnish

○ Heat the butter and oil in the soup maker using the sauté function. Add the onion and potatoes and sauté for 5 minutes, stirring frequently with a wooden spatula.

○ Stir in the flour and cook for 1 minute, then gradually add the milk, stirring constantly.

○ Add half the sweetcorn, then cook on the Smooth setting.

○ Stir the remaining sweetcorn and cream into the soup and season to taste. Serve in warm bowls, sprinkled with crumbled crispy bacon.

CHICKPEA AND CHESTNUT

SERVES 4

1 tablespoon olive oil

2 celery sticks, diced

2 garlic cloves, finely chopped

1 red chilli, deseeded and diced

1 teaspoon finely chopped rosemary

400 g (13 oz) can chopped tomatoes

400 g (13 oz) pack cooked peeled chestnuts

400 g (13 oz) can chickpeas, rinsed and drained

400 ml (14 fl oz) vegetable stock

salt and pepper

TO SERVE

2 tablespoons olive oil

2 tablespoons grated Parmesan cheese

○ Heat the oil in the soup maker using the sauté function. Add the celery, garlic, chilli and rosemary and sauté for 2–3 minutes, stirring frequently with a wooden spatula.

○ Stir in the tomatoes, chestnuts and chickpeas, then pour in the stock, stir, and cook on the Smooth setting.

○ Season the soup to taste, then serve in warm bowls, drizzled with the olive oil and sprinkled with the Parmesan.

SWEET POTATO, SQUASH AND COCONUT

SERVES 4

2 sweet potatoes, peeled and cut into chunks

1 butternut squash, peeled, deseeded and cut into chunks

1 onion, diced

2 garlic cloves, peeled

1 teaspoon cumin seeds

2 tablespoons olive oil

½ teaspoon dried chilli flakes, plus extra to garnish (optional)

900 ml (1½ pints) vegetable stock

200 ml (7 fl oz) coconut cream

1 teaspoon garam masala

salt and pepper

toast, to serve

○ Preheat the oven to 200°C (400°F), Gas Mark 6. Place the sweet potatoes, squash, onion and garlic on a baking sheet. Sprinkle over the cumin seeds and drizzle with the oil. Roast for 25–30 minutes until tender and golden.

○ Spoon the roasted vegetables into the soup maker, then add the remaining ingredients. Cook on the Smooth setting.

○ Pour the soup into warm bowls and sprinkle with a pinch of chilli flakes. Serve with toast.

PUMPKIN AND APPLE

SERVES 4

2 tomatoes

2 tablespoons olive oil

1 onion, diced

600 g (1¼ lb) pumpkin, cut into chunks

1 Bramley apple, peeled, cored and diced

900 ml (1½ pints) vegetable stock

100 ml (3½ fl oz) Greek yogurt

salt and pepper

1 tablespoon chopped parsley, to garnish

○ Place the tomatoes in a heatproof bowl and pour over boiling water to cover. Leave for 1–2 minutes, then drain, cut a cross at the stem end of each tomato and peel off the skins. Roughly dice and set aside.

○ Heat the oil in the soup maker using the sauté function. Add the onion and sauté for 3–4 minutes until beginning to soften, stirring frequently with a wooden spatula. Add the pumpkin and stir to coat with the onions.

○ Stir in the apple and tomatoes. Pour in the stock, then cook on the Smooth setting for 10 minutes. Add the yogurt and continue to cook on the Smooth setting.

○ Season the soup to taste, then serve in warm bowls, sprinkled with the chopped parsley.

SERVES 4

50 g (2 oz) unsalted butter

½ tablespoon olive oil

1 large onion, diced

2 smoked garlic cloves, crushed

750 g (1½ lb) floury potatoes, peeled and diced

1 litre (1¾ pints) vegetable stock

½ teaspoon smoked sea salt

125 ml (4 fl oz) milk

4 tablespoons fresh herbs, such as parsley, thyme and chives, plus extra snipped chives to garnish

pepper

Greek yogurt, to serve

POTATO AND SMOKED GARLIC

O Heat the butter and oil in the soup maker using the sauté function. Add the onion and smoked garlic and sauté for 3–4 minutes until beginning to soften, stirring frequently with a wooden spatula. Stir in the potatoes and cook for another 4–5 minutes, stirring frequently.

O Pour in the stock and season with the smoked sea salt and pepper. Cook on the Smooth setting for 10 minutes. Add the milk and continue to cook on Smooth.

O Stir in the herbs and season the soup to taste.

O Pour into warm bowls, then top with spoonfuls of yogurt and garnish with the remaining chives and freshly ground black pepper.

SERVES 4

50 g (2 oz) butter

½ tablespoon olive oil

1 onion, diced

3 dessert apples, peeled, cored and diced

pinch of cayenne pepper (or to taste), plus extra to garnish

400 g (13 oz) floury potatoes, peeled and diced

750 ml (1¼ pints) vegetable stock

300 ml (½ pint) milk

salt and pepper

FOR THE APPLE GARNISH

15 g (½ oz) butter

½–1 dessert apple, peeled, cored and diced

SPICY APPLE AND POTATO

○ Melt the butter and oil in the soup maker using the sauté function. Add the onion and sauté for 5 minutes until softened, stirring frequently with a wooden spatula. Add the apples, cayenne and potatoes and cook, stirring, for another 2 minutes.

○ Pour in the stock and milk, then cook on the Smooth setting.

○ Meanwhile, make the apple garnish. Melt the butter in a small frying pan, add the diced apple and cook over a high heat until crisp and golden.

○ Serve the soup in warm bowls, garnished with the diced apple and a sprinkling of cayenne pepper.

SPICY SWEET POTATO AND RED PEPPER

SERVES 4

2 tablespoons vegetable oil

1 red onion, diced

1 red pepper, cored, deseeded and diced

550 g (1 lb) sweet potatoes, peeled and diced

¼ teaspoon ground cumin

8 baby tomatoes

1.2 litres (2 pints) vegetable stock

25 g (1 oz) creamed coconut, chopped

salt and pepper

natural yogurt, to serve

coriander sprigs, to garnish

○ Heat the oil in the soup maker using the sauté function. Add the onion and red pepper and sauté for 3–4 minutes, stirring frequently with a wooden spatula. Stir in the sweet potatoes, cumin and tomatoes and cook, stirring, for another 2–3 minutes.

○ Pour in the stock, then cook on the Smooth setting for 6 minutes. Stir in the creamed coconut and continue to cook on Smooth.

○ Season the soup to taste, then serve in warm bowls, topped with dollops of yogurt and coriander sprigs.

SERVES 4

1 tablespoon olive oil

1 leek, trimmed, cleaned and thinly sliced

1 garlic clove, crushed

400 g (13 oz) can Puy lentils, rinsed and drained

1.2 litres (2 pints) vegetable stock

2 tablespoons chopped mixed herbs, such as thyme and parsley

200 g (7 oz) frozen peas

salt and pepper

TO SERVE

2 tablespoons crème fraîche

1 tablespoon chopped mint

LENTIL AND PEA

○ Heat the oil in the soup maker using the sauté function. Add the leek and garlic and sauté for 5–6 minutes until softened, stirring frequently with a wooden spatula.

○ Add the lentils, stock and herbs, then cook on the Chunky setting for 20 minutes. Add the peas and continue to cook on Chunky.

○ Meanwhile, mix together the crème fraîche and mint in a small bowl. Cover and chill.

○ Turn the soup maker off and on again to activate the blender function, if your model requires. Pulse a few times to give the soup a thicker consistency, while still retaining some whole lentils and peas.

○ Season the soup to taste, then serve in warm bowls, with the minty crème fraîche as an optional topping.

SERVES 4

25 g (1 oz) butter

1 tablespoon olive oil

1 onion, diced

1 garlic clove, finely chopped

1 teaspoon ground coriander

½ teaspoon ground cumin

½ teaspoon ground turmeric

500 g (1 lb) parsnips, diced

1 litre (1¾ pints) vegetable stock

50 g (2 oz) dried red lentils

salt and pepper

TO SERVE

125 ml (4 fl oz) double cream

2 tablespoons sweet chilli sauce

SPICED PARSNIP AND RED LENTIL

○ Heat the butter and oil in the soup maker using the sauté function. Add the onion and sauté for 5 minutes until softened, stirring frequently with a wooden spatula. Stir in the garlic and spices and cook, stirring, for another 2 minutes. Add the parsnips and stir to coat with the spices.

○ Pour in the stock and lentils, then cook on the Smooth setting.

○ Season the soup to taste, then serve in warm bowls, drizzled with the cream and sweet chilli sauce.

SUN-DRIED TOMATO AND CHORIZO

SERVES 4

3 tablespoons olive oil

1 red onion, diced

2 garlic cloves, finely chopped

1 teaspoon hot smoked paprika

2 x 400 g (13 oz) cans butter beans, rinsed and drained

100 g (3½ oz) sun-dried tomatoes, drained

500 g (1 lb) passata

900 ml (1½ pints) vegetable stock

150 g (5 oz) chorizo, diced

salt and pepper

chopped parsley, to garnish

crusty bread, to serve

○ Ilustrated on page 56.

○ Heat 2 tablespoons of the oil in the soup maker using the sauté function. Add the onion and garlic and sauté for 4–5 minutes until softened, stirring frequently with a wooden spatula. Add the paprika and butter beans and cook, stirring, for another minute.

○ Add the sun-dried tomatoes, passata and stock, then cook on the Chunky setting.

○ Meanwhile, heat the remaining oil in a small frying pan, add the chorizo and fry for 2–3 minutes until golden, stirring frequently. Remove with a slotted spoon and drain on kitchen paper.

○ Season the soup to taste, then pour into warm bowls. Scatter with the chorizo and parsley and serve with crusty bread.

SERVES 6

1 tablespoon olive oil

1 onion, diced

375 g (12 oz) carrots, diced

375 g (12 oz) sweet potato, peeled and diced

2 garlic cloves, finely chopped

1 teaspoon ground cumin

½ teaspoon hot smoked paprika

1 litre (1¾ pints) vegetable stock

salt and pepper

100 g (3½ oz) feta cheese, crumbled, to serve

chopped mint, to garnish

FOR THE PAPRIKA OIL

3 tablespoons olive oil

¼ teaspoon hot smoked paprika

SMOKY CARROT AND SWEET POTATO

○ Heat the oil in the soup maker using the sauté function. Add the onion and sauté for 5 minutes until softened, stirring frequently with a wooden spatula.

○ Stir in the carrots, sweet potato, garlic, cumin and paprika. Pour in the stock, then cook on the Smooth setting.

○ Meanwhile, make the paprika oil. Mix together the olive oil and paprika in a small bowl and set aside to allow the paprika to infuse the oil.

○ Season the soup to taste, then pour into warm bowls. Drizzle over the paprika oil and sprinkle with the feta. Serve garnished with chopped mint.

SERVES 4

4 tablespoons olive oil, plus extra to serve (optional)

1 aubergine, sliced

1 onion, diced

2 garlic cloves, finely chopped

½ teaspoon smoked paprika

1 teaspoon ground cumin

125 g (4 oz) dried red lentils

400 g (13 oz) can chopped tomatoes

750 ml (1¼ pints) vegetable stock

salt and pepper

chopped coriander leaves, to garnish

toasted ciabatta bread, to serve

TOMATO, LENTIL AND AUBERGINE

○ Heat 1 tablespoon of the oil in the soup maker using the sauté function. Add one-third of the sliced aubergine and sauté on both sides for 1–2 minutes until softened and golden, turning with a wooden spatula. Remove with a slotted spoon and transfer to a plate. Repeat with the remaining aubergine slices, in batches, using another 2 tablespoons of the oil.

○ Add the remaining oil to the soup maker and sauté the onion for 5 minutes until softened, stirring frequently. Stir in the garlic, paprika and cumin and cook for another minute.

○ Stir in the lentils and tomatoes, then return the aubergine slices to the soup maker. Pour in the stock and cook on the Chunky setting.

○ Serve the soup as it is or, alternatively pulse a few times, if your soup maker permits, to give the soup a thicker consistency, while still retaining some chunks.

○ Season the soup to taste, then pour into warm bowls. Drizzle with a little extra olive oil, if liked, and sprinkle with the chopped coriander. Serve with toasted ciabatta bread.

SERVES 4

1 tablespoon olive oil

2 leeks, trimmed, cleaned and thinly sliced

1 cauliflower, core discarded and florets cut into small pieces

600 ml (1 pint) vegetable stock

300 ml (½ pint) milk

2 teaspoons Dijon mustard

1 teaspoon ground nutmeg

100 g (3½ oz) Cheddar cheese, grated

salt and pepper

FOR THE PAPRIKA CROUTONS

3 tablespoons vegetable oil

2 thick slices of white or brown bread, cut into small cubes

1 teaspoon paprika

CAULIFLOWER CHEESE

○ Heat the olive oil in the soup maker using the sauté function. Add the leeks and sauté for 5–6 minutes until softened, stirring frequently with a wooden spatula.

○ Add the cauliflower florets, stock and milk, then cook on the Smooth setting for 10 minutes. Add the mustard, nutmeg, cheese and seasoning and continue to cook on Smooth.

○ Meanwhile, make the croutons. Heat the vegetable oil in a large, heavy-based frying pan over a high heat. Toss the bread cubes with the paprika, then add to the frying pan and cook, stirring frequently, for 2–3 minutes until golden and crisp. Remove with a slotted spoon and drain on kitchen paper.

○ Serve the soup in warm bowls, sprinkled with the croutons.

SERVES 4

1 tablespoon olive oil

2 onions, diced

2 garlic cloves, finely chopped

4 rindless lean back bacon rashers, diced

500 g (1 lb) sweet potatoes, peeled and diced

2 parsnips, diced

1 teaspoon chopped thyme

900 ml (1½ pints) vegetable stock

50 g (2 oz) butter

1 baby Savoy cabbage, finely shredded

salt and pepper

Irish soda bread, to serve

SWEET POTATO AND CABBAGE

○ Heat the oil in the soup maker using the sauté function. Add the onions, garlic and bacon and sauté for 5 minutes until the onions are softened, stirring frequently with a wooden spatula. Add the sweet potatoes, parsnips and thyme and cook for another 2–3 minutes, stirring frequently.

○ Pour in the stock, then cook on the Smooth setting.

○ Meanwhile, melt the butter in a frying pan, add the cabbage and stir-fry until soft. Stir into the cooked soup and season to taste.

○ Serve in warm bowls with Irish soda bread.

SERVES 4

1 tablespoon olive oil

1 onion, diced

500 g (1 lb) pumpkin or butternut squash, peeled, deseeded and diced

2 carrots, diced

40 g (1½ oz) quinoa

2 teaspoons harissa paste, plus extra to serve

1 litre (1¾ pints) vegetable stock

salt and pepper

handful of coriander leaves, roughly chopped, to garnish

PUMPKIN, CARROT AND QUINOA

○ Heat the oil in the soup maker using the sauté function. Add the onion and sauté for 4–5 minutes until softened, stirring frequently with a wooden spatula. Add the pumpkin or squash, carrots, quinoa and harissa and stir to coat the vegetables with the harissa paste.

○ Pour in the stock, then cook on the Chunky setting to retain a thick consistency.

○ Season the soup to taste, then serve in warm bowls, topped with a little extra harissa and sprinkled with chopped coriander.

LENTIL, MUSTARD AND CHICKPEA

SERVES 4

1 tablespoon olive or coconut oil

¼ teaspoon mustard seeds

½ teaspoon ground cumin

½ teaspoon ground turmeric

1 small onion, diced

1.5 cm (¾ inch) piece of fresh root ginger, peeled and finely chopped

1 garlic clove, finely chopped

100 g (3½ oz) dried red lentils

250 g (8 oz) canned chickpeas, rinsed and drained

900 ml (1½ pints) vegetable stock

50 g (2 oz) baby spinach leaves

salt and pepper

○ Heat the oil in the soup maker using the sauté function. Add the dried spices and when the mustard seeds start to pop, add the onion, ginger and garlic. Sauté for 4–5 minutes until softened, stirring frequently with a wooden spatula.

○ Add the lentils and chickpeas and stir well to coat. Pour in the stock, then cook on the Chunky setting.

○ Pulse the soup maker a few times, if your machine permits, to give the soup a thicker consistency, while still retaining some of the chickpeas and lentils.

○ Stir the spinach into the soup until wilted and season to taste. Serve in warm bowls.

SERVES 6

2 tablespoons sunflower oil

1 onion, diced

2 garlic cloves, finely chopped

4 teaspoons mild curry paste

2.5 cm (1 inch) piece of fresh root ginger, peeled and grated

2 small baking potatoes, peeled and diced

2 carrots, diced

1 small cauliflower, core discarded and florets cut into small pieces

75 g (3 oz) dried red lentils

1 litre (1¾ pints) vegetable or chicken stock

400 g (13 oz) can chopped tomatoes

200 g (7 oz) spinach leaves, larger leaves torn into pieces

salt and pepper

naan breads, to serve (optional)

ready-made raita (optional)

CHEAT'S CURRIED VEGETABLE

○ Heat the oil in the soup maker using the sauté function. Add the onion and sauté for 5 minutes until softened, stirring frequently with a wooden spatula. Stir in the garlic, curry paste and ginger and cook for another minute.

○ Add the potatoes, carrots, cauliflower and lentils. Pour in the stock and tomatoes, then cook on the Chunky setting for 10 minutes.

○ Stir the spinach into the soup until wilted and season to taste, then pour into warm bowls. Top with spoonfuls of raita and serve with warmed naan breads, if liked.

SERVES 4

1 tablespoon olive oil

1 large onion, diced

4 garlic cloves, finely chopped

2 celery sticks, diced

1 carrot, diced

400 g (13 oz) can peeled cherry tomatoes

8 ready-to-eat slow-roasted tomatoes (not in oil), diced

400 g (13 oz) can mixed beans, rinsed and drained

1 tablespoon chopped oregano

900 ml (1½ pints) vegetable stock

salt and pepper

TO SERVE

4 tablespoons ricotta cheese

1 tablespoon pesto or basil oil (optional)

crusty French bread

TOMATO AND ITALIAN BEAN

○ Heat the oil in the soup maker using the sauté function. Add the onion, garlic, celery and carrot and sauté for 7–8 minutes until softened and lightly browned, stirring with a wooden spatula.

○ Add the remaining ingredients, then cook on the Smooth setting.

○ Season the soup to taste, then pour into warm bowls. Top with spoonfuls of ricotta and drizzle over the pesto or basil oil, if liked. Serve with crusty French bread.

SPICED VEGETABLE AND CHICKPEA

SERVES 4

2 tablespoons olive or vegetable oil

1 onion, diced

1 green or red pepper, cored, deseeded and diced

1 aubergine, diced

2 teaspoons peeled and diced fresh root ginger

1 teaspoon dried chilli flakes

6 tomatoes, roughly diced

900 ml (1½ pints) vegetable stock

400 g (13 oz) can chickpeas, rinsed and drained

salt and pepper

○ Heat the oil in the soup maker using the sauté function. Add the onion, green or red pepper, aubergine and ginger and sauté for 7–8 minutes until slightly softened, stirring frequently with a wooden spatula.

○ Add the chilli flakes, tomatoes, stock and chickpeas, then cook on the Smooth setting.

○ Season the soup to taste, then serve in mugs.

CHICKEN AND SPINACH CHOWDER

SERVES 4–6

1 tablespoon sunflower oil

25 g (1 oz) butter

4 rindless smoked back bacon rashers, diced

2 small leeks, trimmed, cleaned and thinly sliced

750 g (1½ lb) potatoes, peeled and diced

900 ml (1½ pints) chicken stock

150 g (5 oz) cooked chicken, cut into bite-sized pieces

300 ml (½ pint) semi-skimmed milk

100 g (3½ oz) spinach leaves, roughly chopped

pinch of grated nutmeg

100 ml (3½ fl oz) double cream

salt and pepper

crusty bread, to serve

○ Heat the oil and butter in the soup maker using the sauté function. Add the bacon, leeks and potatoes and sauté for 5–6 minutes, stirring frequently with a wooden spatula.

○ Add the stock, chicken and milk, then cook on the Chunky setting.

○ Stir the spinach into the soup until wilted, then add a little nutmeg and the cream and season to taste. Serve in warm bowls with crusty bread.

CURRIED CHICKPEA AND BUTTERNUT SQUASH

SERVES 4

1 tablespoon olive oil

1 onion, diced

400 g (13 oz) can chickpeas, rinsed and drained

850 g (1¾ lb) butternut squash, peeled, deseeded and diced

1 teaspoon mild curry powder

900 ml (1½ pints) vegetable stock

50 g (2 oz) creamed coconut, chopped

1 teaspoon cumin seeds

salt and pepper

○ Heat 1 tablespoon of the oil in the soup maker using the sauté function. Add the onion and sauté for 5 minutes until softened, stirring frequently with a wooden spatula.

○ Add the chickpeas, squash and curry powder and stir well to coat the vegetables with the spice. Stir in the stock and creamed coconut, then cook on the Smooth setting.

○ Season to taste and serve in warm bowls.

GARLICKY AUBERGINE AND SPINACH

SERVES 4

2 tablespoons olive oil

1 onion, diced

1 aubergine, diced

200 g (7 oz) potato, peeled and diced

2 garlic cloves, finely chopped

1 teaspoon ground cumin

1 teaspoon ground coriander

100 g (3½ oz) canned green lentils, drained

juice of 1 lemon

1 litre (1¾ pints) vegetable stock

125 g (4 oz) young spinach leaves, larger leaves torn into pieces

salt and pepper

crusty bread, to serve (optional)

○ Heat the oil in the soup maker using the sauté function. Add the onion and aubergine and sauté for 5 minutes until softened, stirring frequently with a wooden spatula.

○ Stir in the potato, garlic and ground spices, lentils and lemon juice, then pour in the stock. Cook on the Chunky setting.

○ Stir the spinach leaves into the soup until wilted and season to taste. Serve in warm bowls with warm crusty bread, if liked.

TOMATO RISONI

SERVES 4

4 large tomatoes

2 tablespoons olive oil, plus extra
to serve

1 large onion, diced

2 celery sticks, diced

900 ml (1½ pints) vegetable stock

125 g (4 oz) dried risoni or orzo, or
any tiny dried pasta shapes

6 tablespoons finely chopped flat
leaf parsley

salt and pepper

O Place the tomatoes in a heatproof bowl and pour over boiling water to cover. Leave for 1–2 minutes, then drain, cut a cross at the stem end of each tomato and peel off the skins and discard. Deseed and chop the flesh, then set aside.

O Heat the oil in the soup maker using the sauté function. Add the onion and celery and sauté for 6–8 minutes until softened, stirring frequently with a wooden spatula.

O Add the chopped tomatoes and stock, then cook on the Chunky setting for 15 minutes. Add the risoni, orzo or dried pasta and continue to cook on Chunky.

O Stir in the parsley and season the soup to taste. Serve in warm bowls, drizzled with olive oil.

SERVES 4–6

2 tablespoons olive oil

3 rindless smoked back bacon rashers, diced

2 onions, diced

625 g (1¼ lb) potatoes, peeled and cut into 1 cm (½ inch) cubes

1.2 litres (2 pints) chicken stock

50 g (2 oz) Gruyère cheese, grated

1 tablespoon medium-dry sherry

1 teaspoon Worcestershire sauce

3 tablespoons finely chopped flat leaf parsley (optional)

salt and pepper

TO SERVE (OPTIONAL)

grilled cheese on toast

Worcestershire sauce

GRUYÈRE, BACON AND POTATO

○ Heat the oil in the soup maker using the sauté function. Add the bacon and onions and cook for 5 minutes until softened, stirring frequently with a wooden spatula. Add the potatoes and cook for another 3–4 minutes, stirring frequently.

○ Pour in the stock, then cook on the Chunky setting for 20 minutes. Stir in the cheese, sherry and Worcestershire sauce and continue to cook on Chunky.

○ Turn the soup maker off and on again to activate the blender function. Pulse a few times to give the soup a thicker consistency. Stir the parsley into the soup, if using, and season to taste.

○ Serve in warm bowls with grilled cheese on toast, sprinkled with a little Worcestershire sauce, if liked.

SERVES 4

2 tablespoons olive oil

2 red onions, diced

2 garlic cloves, finely chopped

2 teaspoons brown sugar

625 g (1¼ lb) tomatoes, skinned, if liked
(see page 70), and roughly chopped

2 teaspoons harissa paste

3 teaspoons tomato purée

400 g (13 oz) can chickpeas, rinsed and
drained

900 ml (1½ pints) vegetable or chicken
stock

salt and pepper

ONION, TOMATO AND CHICKPEA

○ Heat the oil in the soup maker using the sauté function. Add the onions and sauté for 5 minutes until the onion is softened, stirring frequently with a wooden spatula. Stir in the garlic and sugar and cook for another 5 minutes, stirring more frequently as the onions begin to caramelize. Stir in the tomatoes and harissa and cook for 5 minutes, stirring frequently.

○ Stir in the tomato purée, chickpeas and stock, then cook on the Chunky setting, retaining some of the whole chickpeas.

○ Season the soup to taste, then serve in warm bowls.

SERVES 4

1 tablespoon olive oil

1 onion, diced

1 garlic clove, crushed

1 red chilli, deseeded and diced

bunch of fresh coriander, stalks and leaves chopped separately, 4 leaves reserved for garnish

1 green pepper, cored, deseeded and diced

1 teaspoon ground cumin

1 teaspoon smoked paprika

2 x 400 g (13 oz) cans black-eyed beans, rinsed and drained

400 g (13 oz) can chopped tomatoes

2 tablespoons sun-dried tomato purée

900 ml (1½ pints) vegetable stock

ready-made guacamole, to serve

salt and pepper

SPICY SALSA

○ Heat the oil in the soup maker using the sauté function. Add the onion, garlic and chilli and sauté for 4 minutes, stirring frequently with a wooden spatula. Add the coriander stalks and green pepper and cook for another 2–3 minutes, then stir in the cumin and paprika.

○ Stir in the beans, tomatoes, tomato purée and stock, then cook on the Chunky setting.

○ Turn the soup maker off and on again to activate the blender function. Pulse a few times to give the soup a thicker consistency, while still retaining some chunks.

○ Stir in the chopped coriander leaves. Season the soup to taste.

○ Serve in warm bowls, garnished with coriander leaves and a dollop of guacamole. .

SERVES 4

1 kg (2 lb) butternut squash, peeled, deseeded and cut into 1 cm (½ inch) cubes

2 tablespoons olive oil

1 tablespoon chopped sage

2 tablespoons pumpkin seeds

1 onion, diced

1 garlic clove, finely chopped

½ tablespoon mild curry powder

2 tablespoons cashew nuts

900 ml (1½ pints) vegetable stock

200 g (7 oz) natural yogurt

salt and pepper

ROASTED BUTTERNUT SQUASH, SAGE AND CASHEW

○ Preheat the oven to 200°C (400°F), Gas Mark 6. Place the squash in a roasting tray and toss with 1 tablespoon of the oil and the sage. Roast for 18–20 minutes until tender and golden, tossing halfway through the cooking.

○ Meanwhile, heat a nonstick frying pan over a medium-low heat and dry-fry the pumpkin seeds for 2–3 minutes until slightly golden and toasted, stirring frequently. Set aside.

○ Heat the remaining oil in the soup maker using the sauté function. Add the onion and garlic and sauté for 4–5 minutes until softened, stirring frequently with a wooden spatula. Add the curry powder and cook, stirring, for another minute.

○ Add the roasted squash, cashew nuts and stock, then cook on the Smooth setting for 10 minutes. Stir in the yogurt, then continue to cook on Smooth.

○ Season the soup to taste, then serve in warm bowls sprinkled with the toasted pumpkin seeds.

SERVES 4

2 tablespoons vegetable oil

1 onion, diced

125 g (4 oz) chorizo, finely diced

1 red pepper, cored, deseeded and diced

1 garlic clove, finely chopped

1 teaspoon ground cumin

1.2 litres (2 pints) chicken stock

2 x 400 g (13 oz) cans black beans, rinsed and drained

salt and pepper

TO SERVE

2 tablespoons lime juice

4 tablespoons soured cream

handful of coriander leaves, chopped

1 red chilli, chopped

CHORIZO AND BLACK BEAN

○ Heat the oil in the soup maker using the sauté function. Add the onion, chorizo, red pepper and garlic and sauté for 6–8 minutes, stirring frequently with a wooden spatula.

○ Stir in the cumin, then add the stock and beans and cook on the Chunky setting.

○ If required, turn the soup maker off and on again to activate the blender function. Pulse for a few seconds to give the soup a thicker consistency, while still retaining some chunks.

○ Season the soup to taste, then pour into warm bowls. Drizzle over a little lime juice and top with the soured cream. Serve sprinkled with the chopped coriander and chilli.

SERVES 6

2 tablespoons olive oil

1 onion, diced

2 garlic cloves, finely chopped

1 tablespoon peeled and diced fresh root ginger

2 teaspoons mild curry powder

1 teaspoon garam masala

½ teaspoon ground turmeric

125 g (4 oz) dried red lentils

875 g (1¾ lb) parsnips, diced

1.2 litres (2 pints) vegetable stock

200 ml (7 fl oz) coconut milk

salt and pepper

naan bread, to serve

CURRIED PARSNIP AND LENTIL

○ Heat the oil in the soup maker using the sauté function. Add the onion, garlic and ginger and sauté for 4–5 minutes until softened, stirring frequently with a wooden spatula. Add the spices, lentils and parsnips and cook for another 2–3 minutes, stirring frequently.

○ Pour in the vegetable stock and coconut milk, then cook on the Smooth setting.

○ Season the soup to taste, then serve in warm bowls with warm naan bread.

ALL-TIME CLASSICS

HADDOCK AND BACON CHOWDER

SERVES 4

25 g (1 oz) butter

1 tablespoon olive oil

1 onion, diced

300 g (10 oz) potatoes, peeled and diced

4 rindless smoked streaky bacon rashers, diced

750 ml (1¼ pints) fish stock

125 g (4 oz) frozen sweetcorn, thawed

500 g (1 lb) smoked haddock, skinned and cut into bite-sized chunks

150 ml (¼ pint) double cream

salt and pepper

chopped parsley, to garnish

○ Illustrated on page 78.

○ Heat the butter and oil in the soup maker using the sauté function. Add the onion, potatoes and bacon and sauté for 6–8 minutes until just beginning to brown, stirring frequently with a wooden spatula.

○ Add the stock, sweetcorn and smoked haddock, making sure the fish is below the surface of the stock. Cook on the Chunky setting.

○ Stir the cream into the soup and season to taste. Serve in warm bowls, sprinkled with parsley.

SERVES 4

50 g (2 oz) butter

1 tablespoon olive oil

2 leeks, trimmed, cleaned and thinly sliced

2 garlic cloves, finely chopped

750 g (1½ lb) floury potatoes, peeled and diced

1.2 litres (2 pints) vegetable or chicken stock

100 g (3½ oz) strong Stilton or other blue cheese, rind removed and cheese crumbled

100 ml (3½ fl oz) single cream

salt and pepper

1 tablespoon chopped chives, to garnish

crusty bread, to serve

STILTON, POTATO AND LEEK

○ Heat the butter and oil in the soup maker using the sauté function. Add the leeks and garlic and sauté for 5–6 minutes until softened, stirring frequently with a wooden spatula. Add the potatoes and cook, stirring, for another 1–2 minutes.

○ Pour in the stock, then cook on the Smooth setting.

○ Add the cheese and cream to the soup and stir until melted, then season to taste.

○ Pour into warm bowls, garnish with the chives and serve with crusty bread.

SERVES 4

1 kg (2 lb) ripe tomatoes, halved

4 garlic cloves, unpeeled

2 tablespoons olive oil

1 onion, diced

1 carrot, diced

1 celery stick, diced

1 red pepper, cored, deseeded and diced

700 ml (1¼ pints) vegetable stock

salt and pepper

4 tablespoons grated Parmesan cheese, to serve

ROASTED TOMATO

○ Preheat the oven to 200°C (400°F), Gas Mark 6. Place the tomato halves and garlic in a roasting tray. Sprinkle with 1 tablespoon of the oil and some pepper and roast for 20 minutes.

○ Heat the remaining oil using the sauté function. Add the onion, carrot, celery and red pepper and sauté for 5–6 minutes until softened, stirring frequently with a wooden spatula.

○ When the tomatoes are cooked, remove the garlic from the tray and squeeze the flesh into the soup maker, then add the roasted tomatoes and any juices.

○ Pour in the stock, then cook on the Smooth setting.

○ Season the soup to taste, then serve in warm bowls, sprinkled with the Parmesan.

SERVES 4

1 tablespoon sunflower oil

1 onion, diced

900 ml (1½ pints) chicken stock

150 ml (¼ pint) milk

1 large potato, peeled and diced

375 g (12 oz) canned sweetcorn, drained

2 cooked chicken breasts, shredded

salt and pepper

crispy bacon pieces (see page 34), to garnish

CHICKEN AND SWEETCORN

- Heat the oil in the soup maker using the sauté function. Add the onion and sauté for 5 minutes until softened, stirring frequently with a wooden spatula.

- Add the stock, milk, potato and sweetcorn, then cook on the Chunky setting.

- Turn the soup maker off and on again to activate the blender function. Pulse a few times to give the soup a thicker consistency, while still retaining some chunks.

- Stir the shredded chicken into the soup and season to taste. Serve in warm bowls, sprinkled with bacon bits.

SERVES 6

25 g (1 oz) butter

½ tablespoon olive oil

1 onion, diced

500 g (1 lb) potatoes, peeled and diced

300 g (10 oz) boneless smoked haddock fillet

900 ml (1½ pints) fish stock

150 ml (¼ pint) milk

6 tablespoons double cream

salt and pepper

chopped flat leaf parsley, to garnish

toasted barley bannocks or soda griddle scones, to serve

CULLEN SKINK

○ Preheat the oven to 190°C (375°F), Gas Mark 5. Place the smoked haddock fillet on a foil-lined roasting tray and bake for 10-15 minutes.

○ Heat the butter and oil in the soup maker using the sauté function. Add the onion and sauté for 5 minutes until softened, stirring frequently with a wooden spatula. Stir in the potatoes and cook for another 5 minutes.

○ Once the haddock is cooked, add two thirds of the fillet to the soup maker, retaining a third to garnish. Pour in the stock, milk and cream and cook on the Smooth setting.

○ Season the soup to taste, then pour into warm bowls. Top with the remaining fish and sprinkle with the chopped parsley. Serve with toasted barley bannocks or soda griddle scones.

SERVES 4

1 tablespoon butter

½ tablespoon olive oil

1 onion, diced

1 potato, peeled and diced

1 litre (1¾ pints) vegetable stock

400 g (13 oz) frozen peas

6 tablespoons mint leaves, finely chopped, plus extra sprigs to garnish

salt and pepper

crème fraîche, to serve

MINTED PEA

○ Heat the butter and oil in the soup maker using the sauté function. Add the onion and potato and sauté for 5 minutes, stirring frequently with a wooden spatula.

○ Add the stock and peas, then cook on the Smooth setting for 10 minutes. Add the mint and continue to cook on Smooth.

○ Season the soup to taste, then serve in warm bowls with dollops of crème fraîche and mint sprigs to garnish.

CHUNKY MUSHROOM

SERVES 4

25 g (1 oz) butter

½ tablespoon olive oil

1 large onion, diced

1 leek, trimmed, cleaned and thinly sliced

2 garlic cloves, crushed

300 g (10 oz) chestnut mushrooms, roughly diced

2 tablespoons plain flour

500 ml (17 fl oz) vegetable stock

400 ml (14 fl oz) milk

1 tablespoon finely chopped tarragon

salt and pepper

crusty bread, to serve

○ Heat the butter and oil in the soup maker using the sauté function. Add the onion, leek and garlic and sauté for 3–4 minutes until beginning to soften, stirring frequently with a wooden spatula. Stir in the mushrooms until well combined, then cook, stirring, for another 2–3 minutes.

○ Stir in the flour and cook for 1 minute. Pour in the stock a little at a time, stirring well between each addition. When all the stock is added, pour in the milk, then cook on the Chunky setting.

○ Stir the chopped tarragon into the soup and season to taste. Serve in warm bowls with crusty bread.

OLD ENGLISH PEA AND HAM

SERVES 4

1 tablespoon olive oil

2 onions, diced

2 celery sticks, diced

1 carrot, diced

3 x 300 g (10 oz) cans marrowfat peas, drained

900 ml (1½ pints) ham or chicken stock

1 teaspoon English mustard

250 g (8 oz) piece of cooked ham, cut into bite-sized pieces

4 tablespoons chopped parsley

salt and pepper

crusty bread, to serve

○ Heat the oil in in the soup maker using the sauté function. Add the onion, celery and carrot and sauté for 6–8 minutes until softened, stirring frequently with a wooden spatula.

○ Add the peas, stock and mustard, then cook on the Smooth or Chunky setting, whichever you prefer (the soup pictured above was prepared using the Chunky setting).

○ Stir the ham and parsley into the soup and season to taste. Serve in warm bowls with crusty bread.

CREAMY CHICKEN AND MUSHROOM

SERVES 4

2 tablespoons olive or vegetable oil

1 onion, diced

1 celery stick or leek, diced

400 g (13 oz) mushrooms, diced

900 ml (1½ pints) chicken or vegetable stock

225 g (7½ oz) cooked chicken, shredded

50 ml (2 fl oz) single or double cream

salt and pepper

crusty bread, to serve (optional)

○ Heat the oil in the soup maker using the sauté function. Add the onion and celery or leek and sauté for 5 minutes until softened, stirring frequently with a wooden spatula. Add the mushrooms and cook for another 3–4 minutes until softened, stirring frequently.

○ Pour in the chicken or vegetable stock, then cook on the Smooth setting.

○ Stir the shredded chicken and cream into the soup and season to taste. Serve in mugs with crusty bread, if liked.

SPICY TOMATO AND BEAN

SERVES 4

1 tablespoon olive oil

1 onion, diced

2 garlic cloves, finely chopped

½ teaspoon hot smoked paprika

2 teaspoons light muscovado sugar

½ teaspoon dried oregano

1 tablespoon tomato purée

625 g (1¼ lb) tomatoes, skinned, if liked (see page 70) and cut into chunks

400 g (13 oz) can cannellini beans, rinsed and drained

750 ml (1¼ pints) vegetable stock

salt and pepper

warm garlic bread, to serve

○ Heat the oil in the soup maker using the sauté function. Add the onion and sauté for 4–5 minutes until the onion is lightly browned, stirring frequently with a wooden spatula. Stir in the garlic and paprika and cook, stirring, for a further minute.

○ Add the sugar, oregano, tomato purée, tomatoes and cannellini beans, then pour in the stock and cook on the Chunky setting.

○ Season the soup to taste, then serve in warm bowls with warm garlic bread.

SPICED BUTTERNUT SQUASH

SERVES 4

1 tablespoon olive oil

500 g (1 lb) butternut squash, peeled, deseeded and diced

250 g (8 oz) parsnips, diced

250 g (8 oz) celeriac, peeled and diced

2 teaspoons ground cumin

2 teaspoons ginger purée from a jar or tube

1.2 litres (2 pints) vegetable stock

salt and pepper

4 tablespoons crème fraîche, to serve

chopped flat leaf parsley, to garnish

○ Heat the oil in the soup maker using the sauté function. Add the squash, parsnips and celeriac and sauté for 5–6 minutes, stirring frequently with a wooden spatula. Stir in the cumin and ginger.

○ Pour in the vegetable stock, then cook on the Smooth setting.

○ Season the soup to taste, then pour into warm bowls. Top with spoonfuls of crème fraîche and serve sprinkled with flat leaf parsley.

SERVES 4

50 g (2 oz) butter

½ tablespoon olive oil

3 large onions, halved and thinly sliced

2 garlic cloves, roughly chopped

1 tablespoon plain flour

900 ml (1½ pints) beef stock

1 teaspoon dried thyme or 2 teaspoons chopped thyme leaves

salt and pepper

FOR THE CHEESY CROUTES

8 slices of French baguette

100 g (3½ oz) Emmental or Cheddar cheese, finely grated

FRENCH ONION WITH CHEESY CROUTES

○ Heat the butter and oil in the soup maker using the sauté function. Add the onions and cook for 12–14 minutes until soft and golden, stirring frequently with a wooden spatula. Add the garlic and cook for another 4–5 minutes until the onion takes on a deeper golden colour.

○ Stir in the flour and cook for 1 minute. Stir in the stock a little at a time, stirring well between each addition. Add the thyme and then cook on the Chunky setting.

○ Meanwhile, make the croutes. Top the baguette slices with the grated cheese. Cook under a preheated medium-hot grill for 2–3 minutes until the cheese is melting and golden.

○ Season the soup to taste, then serve in warm bowls, topped with the cheesy croutes.

SERVES 4–6

100 g (3½ oz) plum tomatoes

2 tablespoons olive oil, plus extra to serve

1 onion, diced

1 carrot, diced

2 celery sticks, diced

2 garlic cloves, peeled and finely chopped

1 potato, peeled and diced

125 g (4 oz) peas or broad beans, thawed if frozen

1 courgette, diced

75 g (3 oz) green beans, trimmed and cut into 3.5 cm (1½ inch) pieces

1 litre (1¾ pints) vegetable stock

75 g (3 oz) small dried pasta shapes

10 basil leaves, torn

salt and pepper

TO SERVE

grated Parmesan cheese

toasted country bread

SPRING MINESTRONE

○ Place the tomatoes in a heatproof bowl and pour over boiling water to cover. Leave for 1–2 minutes, then drain, cut a cross at the stem end of each tomato and peel off the skins. Chop the flesh, then set aside.

○ Heat the oil in the soup maker using the sauté function. Add the onion, carrot, celery and garlic and sauté for 5 minutes, stirring frequently with a wooden spatula. Add the potato, peas or broad beans, courgette and green beans and cook for another 2 minutes, stirring frequently. Add the tomatoes, season with salt and pepper and continue to cook for 2 minutes.

○ Pour in the stock, then cook on the Chunky setting for 15 minutes. Add the pasta and continue to cook on Chunky.

○ Stir the basil into the soup and season to taste.

○ Pour into warm bowls, drizzle with extra olive oil and sprinkle with the Parmesan. Serve with toasted country bread.

SERVES 4

2 tablespoons olive oil

1 onion, diced

6 rindless back bacon rashers, diced

4 tablespoons chopped mint

250 g (8 oz) peeled potatoes, diced

500 g (1 lb) frozen peas

1 litre (1¾ pints) chicken stock

salt and pepper

TO SERVE

4 tablespoons crème fraîche

toasted mixed seeds (see page 37)

PEA, MINT AND BACON

○ Heat the oil in the soup maker using the sauté function, Add the onion and bacon and sauté for 3–5 minutes until the onion is softened and the bacon is browned, stirring frequently with a wooden spatula. Add the mint and potatoes and cook for another minute.

○ Stir in the peas and stock, then cook on the Smooth setting.

○ Season the soup to taste, then pour into warm bowls. Swirl through the crème fraîche and serve sprinkled with toasted seeds on top.

SERVES 4-6

1 tablespoon olive oil

1 onion, diced

1 carrot, diced

1 dessert apple, cored and coarsely grated

2 garlic cloves, finely chopped

400 g (13 oz) can chopped tomatoes

75 g (3 oz) dried red lentils

50 g (2 oz) sultanas

3 teaspoons mild curry paste

900 ml (1½ pints) vegetable or chicken stock

salt and pepper

FOR THE CORIANDER CROUTES

50 g (2 oz) butter, softened

2 garlic cloves, finely chopped

3 tablespoons chopped coriander leaves

8-12 slices of French baguette, depending on size

MULLIGATAWNY WITH CORIANDER CROUTES

○ Heat the oil in the soup maker using the sauté function. Add the onion, carrot, apple and garlic and sauté for 5 minutes until softened, stirring frequently with a wooden spatula.

○ Add the remaining ingredients, then cook on the Chunky setting.

○ Meanwhile, make the croutes. Beat together the butter, garlic and chopped coriander in a bowl. Toast the bread on both sides, then spread with the butter.

○ Season the soup to taste, then serve in warm bowls along with the croutes.

CAULIFLOWER, LEEK AND STILTON

SERVES 4–6

1 tablespoon olive oil

25 g (1 oz) butter

1 large leek, trimmed, cleaned and thinly sliced

2 tablespoons long-grain white rice

1 cauliflower, core discarded and florets cut into small pieces

900 ml (1½ pints) vegetable stock

450 ml (¾ pint) semi-skimmed milk

4 smoked streaky bacon rashers (optional)

125 g (4 oz) Stilton or other blue cheese, crumbled

salt and pepper

○ Heat the oil and butter in the soup maker using the sauté function. Add the leek and sauté for 3–4 minutes, stirring frequently with a wooden spatula.

○ Add the rice, cauliflower, stock and milk, then cook on the Smooth setting.

○ Meanwhile, place the bacon rashers, if using, on a foil-lined grill pan and cook under a preheated grill for 5–6 minutes until crispy and golden, turning occasionally. Chop the grilled bacon into small pieces. Drain on kitchen paper.

○ Stir half the cheese into the soup and season to taste.

○ Pour into warm bowls, then sprinkle over the remaining cheese, the chopped crispy bacon, if using, and some freshly ground black pepper.

SERVES 4

550 g (1 lb) frozen broad beans, thawed

2 tablespoons olive oil

2 shallots, diced

1 large carrot, diced

1 celery stick, diced

900 ml (1½ pints) vegetable stock

1 tablespoon chopped mint leaves

salt and pepper

4 tablespoons double cream, to serve

BROAD BEAN AND MINT

○ Blanch the broad beans in a saucepan of boiling water for 3–4 minutes, then drain and refresh under cold running water. Peel off the tough outer skins.

○ Meanwhile, heat the oil in the soup maker using the sauté function. Add the shallots, carrot and celery and sauté for 5–6 minutes until softened, stirring frequently with a wooden spatula.

○ Stir in the skinned broad beans and pour in the stock, then cook on the Smooth setting for 10 minutes. Stir in the mint and continue to cook on Smooth.

○ Season the soup to taste, then pour into warm bowls. Swirl through the cream before serving.

SERVES 6

3 tablespoons olive oil

2 garlic cloves, crushed

1 red pepper, cored, deseeded and diced

1 onion, diced

250 g (8 oz) tomatoes, finely chopped

1 teaspoon finely chopped thyme

2 x 400 g (14 oz) cans haricot or cannellini beans, rinsed and drained

1.2 litres (2 pints) vegetable stock

2 tablespoons finely chopped flat leaf parsley

salt and pepper

crusty bread, to serve

WHITE BEAN PROVENCAL

○ Heat the oil in the soup maker using the sauté function. Add the garlic, red pepper and onion and sauté for 5 minutes until softened, stirring frequently with a wooden spatula. Add the tomatoes and thyme and cook for another minute.

○ Add the beans and vegetable stock, then cook on the Chunky setting.

○ Stir the parsley into the soup and season to taste. Serve in warm bowls with crusty bread.

SERVES 6

750 g (1½ lb) parsnips, cut into wedges

2 onions, cut into wedges

2 tablespoons olive oil

2 tablespoons clear honey

1 teaspoon turmeric, plus extra to garnish (optional)

1 teaspoon dried chilli flakes

3 garlic cloves, thickly sliced

1.2 litres (2 pints) vegetable or chicken stock

2 tablespoons sherry or cider vinegar

salt and pepper

croutons (see page 14, omitting the garlic), to serve

FOR THE GINGER CREAM

150 ml (¼ pint) double cream

5 cm (2 inch) piece of fresh root ginger, peeled and grated

HONEY-ROASTED PARSNIP WITH GINGER CREAM

○ Preheat the oven to 190°C (375°F), Gas Mark 5. Place the parsnips and onions in a large roasting tray in a single layer, then drizzle with the oil and honey. Sprinkle with the turmeric, chilli flakes and garlic. Roast for 30–40 minutes, turning once, until a deep golden brown with sticky, caramelized edges.

○ Transfer the contents of the roasting tray to the soup maker, scraping all the juicy bits off the bottom of the tray. Pour in the stock and vinegar and season with salt and pepper. Cook on the Smooth setting.

○ Meanwhile, make the ginger cream. Mix together the cream, ginger and a little pepper in a jug.

○ Pour the soup into warm bowls and drizzle over the ginger cream, then sprinkle with a little turmeric, if liked. Serve with croutons.

SERVES 4

1 teaspoon olive oil

2 rindless smoked bacon rashers, diced

2 garlic cloves, crushed

1 onion, diced

a few sprigs of thyme or lemon thyme

2 x 400 g (13 oz) cans cannellini beans, rinsed and drained

900 ml (1½ pints) vegetable stock

salt and pepper

2 tablespoons chopped flat leaf parsley, to garnish

BACON AND WHITE BEAN

○ Heat the oil in the soup maker using the sauté function. Add the bacon, garlic and onion and cook for 3–4 minutes until the bacon is beginning to brown and the onion softens, stirring frequently with a wooden spatula. Add the thyme and cook for another minute.

○ Stir in the beans and stock, then cook on the Smooth setting.

○ Season the soup to taste, then serve in warm bowls, sprinkled with the chopped parsley.

SOMETHING SPECIAL

MINTY CHICKEN AND RICE

SERVES 4

2 tablespoons olive oil

2 onions, diced

1 red chilli, deseeded and finely chopped

1 teaspoon coriander seeds

2 teaspoons dried mint

275 g (9 oz) cooked skinless chicken breast fillets, cut into thin strips

100 g (3½ oz) medium-grain white rice, such as paella, rinsed and drained

2 teaspoons tomato purée

1.2 litres (2 pints) chicken stock

salt and pepper

small bunch of mint, finely shredded, to garnish

lemon wedges, to serve (optional)

○ Illustrated on page 100.

○ Heat the oil in the soup maker using the sauté function. Add the onions, chilli and coriander seeds and sauté for 5 minutes until the onions are softened, stirring frequently with a spatula.

○ Add the dried mint, chicken, rice, tomato purée and stock and mix well, then cook on the Chunky setting.

○ Season the soup to taste, then pour into warm bowls and garnish with the shredded mint. Serve with lemon wedges, if liked.

SERVES 6

25 g (1 oz) butter

1 tablespoon olive oil

4 spring onions, trimmed and thinly sliced

3 fennel bulbs, trimmed, cored and diced, green feathery fronds reserved for garnish

300 g (10 oz) potato, peeled and diced

900 ml (1½ pints) chicken or vegetable stock

75 g (3 oz) Parmesan cheese, coarsely grated

salt and pepper

VELVETY FENNEL AND PARMESAN

○ Heat the butter and oil in the soup maker using the sauté function. Add the spring onions and fennel and sauté for 5 minutes until softened, stirring frequently with a wooden spatula.

○ Stir in the potatoes, stock and 25 g (1 oz) of the cheese, then cook on the Smooth setting.

○ Meanwhile, preheat the oven to 200°C (400°F), Gas Mark 6. Line a baking sheet with nonstick baking paper, then spoon on the remaining grated cheese in 6 well-spaced mounds. Spread each one into a roughly shaped circle about 7.5 cm (3 inches) in diameter. Bake for 5–6 minutes until bubbling and golden brown. Leave to cool on the paper.

○ Season the soup to taste, then pour into cups and garnish with any reserved snipped green fennel fronds. Serve each with a Parmesan wafer, breaking it into pieces and sprinkling over the top of the soup, if liked.

SERVES 4

2 tablespoons sunflower oil

250 g (8 oz) boneless, skinless chicken thighs, diced

4 teaspoons Thai red curry paste

1 teaspoon galangal paste

3 dried kaffir lime leaves

400 ml (14 fl oz) can coconut milk

2 teaspoons Thai fish sauce

1 teaspoon light muscovado sugar

900 ml (1½ pints) chicken stock

4 spring onions, trimmed and thinly sliced, plus 2 to garnish

50 g (2 oz) mangetout, sliced

100 g (3½ oz) bean sprouts, rinsed

salt and pepper

coriander leaves, to garnish

RED CHICKEN AND COCONUT BROTH

○ Heat 1 tablespoon of the oil in a frying pan, add the chicken and cook for 10–12 minutes until browned and nearly cooked through.

○ Heat the remaining oil in the soup maker using the sauté function. Add the cooked chicken and curry paste and cook for 3–4 minutes, stirring frequently with a wooden spoon.

○ Stir in the galangal paste, lime leaves, coconut milk, fish sauce, sugar and stock, then cook on the Chunky setting.

○ Meanwhile, cut very thin strips from the 2 spring onions, then soak in cold water for 10 minutes to create curls. Drain and set aside.

○ Add the remaining spring onions, mangetout and bean sprouts to the soup, then season to taste.

○ Serve in warm bowls, sprinkled with the coriander and spring onion curls.

SERVES 6

25 g (1 oz) butter

1 tablespoon sunflower oil

1 onion, diced

375 g (12 oz) raw beetroot, peeled and diced

2 carrots, diced

2 celery sticks, diced

150 g (5 oz) red cabbage, cored and thinly sliced

300 g (10 oz) potatoes, peeled and diced

2 garlic cloves, finely chopped

1.2 litres (1¾ pints) vegetable or beef stock

1 tablespoon tomato purée

6 tablespoons red wine vinegar

1 tablespoon brown sugar

2 bay leaves

salt and pepper

small bunch of dill, torn, to garnish

200 ml (7 fl oz) soured cream, to serve

RUSSIAN BORSCH

○ Heat the butter and oil in the soup maker using the sauté function. Add the onion and sauté for 5 minutes until softened, stirring frequently with a wooden spatula. Add the beetroot, carrots, celery, red cabbage, potatoes and garlic and cook for another 5 minutes, stirring frequently.

○ Stir in the remaining ingredients, then cook on the Chunky setting.

○ Remove the bay leaves and season the soup to taste.

○ Pour into warm bowls, serve topped with spoonfuls of soured cream, torn dill fronds and a little freshly ground black pepper.

TOMATO, RAS EL HANOUT AND VERMICELLI

SERVES 4

8 large ripe tomatoes

2–3 tablespoons olive oil

4 garlic cloves, chopped

2 onions, diced

2 celery sticks, diced

1 carrot, diced

1–2 teaspoons sugar

1 tablespoon tomato purée

1–2 teaspoons ras el hanout

large bunch of fresh coriander, finely chopped

1.2 litres (2 pints) vegetable stock

100 g (3½ oz) fine vermicelli, broken into small pieces

salt and pepper

crusty bread, to serve (optional)

○ Place the tomatoes in a heatproof bowl and pour over boiling water to cover. Leave for 1–2 minutes, then drain, cut a cross at the stem end of each tomato and peel off the skins. Roughly dice and set aside.

○ Heat the oil in the soup maker using the sauté function. Add the garlic, onions, celery and carrot and sauté for 5 minutes until the vegetables begin to soften, stirring frequently with a wooden spatula. Add the tomatoes and sugar and cook for another 4–5 minutes until the mixture is thick, stirring frequently.

○ Stir in the tomato purée, ras el hanout and most of the coriander, reserving some for garnish. Pour in the stock, then cook on the Chunky setting for 10 minutes. Add the vermicelli and continue to cook on Chunky.

○ Season the soup to taste, then pour into warm bowls and sprinkle with the remaining coriander. Serve with crusty bread, if liked.

SERVES 6

25 g (1 oz) butter

1 tablespoon olive oil

1 onion, diced

2 garlic cloves, finely chopped

350 g (12 oz) potatoes, peeled and diced

1 teaspoon ground cumin

900 ml (1½ pints) vegetable stock

75 g (3 oz) baby spinach leaves

75 g (3 oz) kale, thick stems removed and leaves finely shredded

125 ml (4 fl oz) double cream

salt and pepper

FOR THE BRIE TOASTS

2 oval-shaped rolls, each cut into 3 long slices

150 g (5 oz) Brie cheese, cut into 6 long thin slices

2 tablespoons pistachio nuts, roughly chopped

2 teaspoons clear honey

SMOOTH SPINACH AND KALE WITH BRIE TOASTS

○ Heat the butter and oil in in the soup maker using the sauté function. Add the onion and sauté for 5 minutes until softened, stirring frequently with a wooden spatula. Add the garlic, potatoes and cumin and cook, stirring, for another 2–3 minutes.

○ Pour in the stock, then cook on the Smooth setting for 10 minutes. Add the spinach and kale and continue to cook on Smooth.

○ Meanwhile, make the Brie toasts. Toast the bread on both sides under a preheated grill, then top each with a slice of cheese, a few pistachios and a drizzle of honey. Cook under the hot grill for a few minutes until the cheese is bubbling and the nuts are lightly browned.

○ Stir the cream into the soup and season to taste. Serve in warm bowls with the Brie toasts.

SERVES 4

1 tablespoon sunflower oil

1 onion, diced

1 garlic clove, finely chopped

2 celery sticks, diced

1 carrot, diced

400 g (13 oz) can chopped tomatoes

750 ml (1¼ pints) fish stock

50 g (2 oz) easy-cook long-grain rice

1 bay leaf

2 thyme sprigs

¼ teaspoon dried chilli flakes

75 g (3 oz) okra, sliced

43 g (1½ oz) can dressed brown crab meat

salt and pepper

TO SERVE

170 g (6 oz) can white crab meat (optional)

crusty bread, to serve

CRAB GUMBO

○ Heat the oil in the soup maker using the sauté function. Add the onion and sauté for 5 minutes until softened, stirring frequently with a wooden spatula. Stir in the garlic, celery and carrot and cook for another 2–3 minutes, stirring frequently.

○ Add the tomatoes, stock, rice, herbs, chilli flakes and okra, then cook on the Chunky setting.

○ Remove the bay leaf from the soup, then stir in the brown crab meat and season to taste.

○ Pour into warm bowls and top with the flaked white crab meat, if liked. Serve with warm crusty bread.

PARSNIP, SAGE AND CHESTNUT

HAM AND PEA WITH CRISPY BACON

SERVES 4

3 tablespoons chilli oil, plus extra to serve

20 sage leaves

1 leek, trimmed, cleaned and finely chopped

500 g (1 lb) parsnips, diced

1.2 litres (2 pints) vegetable stock

pinch of ground cloves

200 g (7 oz) pack cooked peeled chestnuts

2 tablespoons lemon juice

salt and pepper

crème fraîche, to serve

○ Heat the chilli oil in the soup maker using the sauté function. Cook the sage leaves, a few at a time, until crisp, then remove with a slotted spoon and drain on kitchen paper.

○ Add the leek and parsnips to the soup maker and sauté for 6-8 minutes until softened, stirring frequently with a wooden spatula.

○ Stir in the stock and cloves, then cook on the Smooth setting for 10 minutes. Add the chestnuts and lemon juice and continue to cook on Smooth.

○ Season to taste and serve in bowls, topped with a little crème fraîche, chilli oil and the crispy sage leaves.

SERVES 4

2 tablespoons olive or vegetable oil

1 large onion, diced

1 large potato, 250 g (8 oz), peeled and diced

2 garlic cloves, finely chopped

300 g (10 oz) frozen peas

1 litre (1¾ pints) ham or vegetable stock

300 g (10 oz) piece of cooked ham, cut into bite-sized pieces

8 rindless streaky bacon rashers

pepper

crusty white bread, to serve

○ Heat the oil in the soup maker using the sauté function. Add the onion, potato and garlic and sauté for 6–7 minutes, stirring frequently with a wooden spatula.

○ Add the peas, stock and ham and season well with pepper. Cook on the Smooth setting.

○ Meanwhile, place the bacon rashers on a foil-lined grill pan and cook under a preheated grill for 5–6 minutes, turning occasionally, until crispy and golden. Chop or crumble the grilled bacon into small pieces. Drain on kitchen paper.

○ Pour the soup into warm bowls and top with the crispy bacon. Serve with crusty white bread.

CHORIZO, FENNEL AND POTATO

SERVES 4–6

2 tablespoons olive oil

1 onion, diced

400 g (13 oz) fennel bulb, trimmed, cored and diced

100 g (3½ oz) chorizo, diced

400 g (13 oz) floury potatoes, peeled and diced

1 litre (1¾ pints) chicken or ham stock

3 tablespoons finely chopped fresh coriander

3 tablespoons crème fraîche

salt and pepper

○ Heat the oil in the soup maker using the sauté function. Add the onion and fennel and sauté for 8–10 minutes until softened, stirring frequently with a wooden spatula.

○ Add the chorizo, potatoes and stock, then cook on the Smooth setting.

○ Stir in the coriander and crème fraîche and season the soup to taste. Serve in small, warm cups.

SAVOY CABBAGE AND PARMESAN

SERVES 4

2 tablespoons olive oil

1 onion, diced

2 garlic cloves, crushed

½ teaspoon fennel seeds

1 Savoy cabbage, finely shredded

1 potato, peeled and diced

1 litre (1¾ pints) vegetable stock

75 g (3 oz) Parmesan cheese, grated, plus 1 tablespoon to serve

salt and pepper

crusty bread, to serve

○ Heat the oil in the soup maker using the sauté function. Add the onion, garlic and fennel seeds and sauté for 3–4 minutes, stirring frequently with a wooden spatula.

○ Add the cabbage, potato and stock, then cook on the Smooth setting for 10 minutes. Stir in the cheese and continue to cook on Smooth.

○ Season the soup to taste, then pour into warm bowls. Sprinkle with the extra Parmesan and serve with crusty bread.

HARISSA-SPICED PEPPER AND CHICKPEA

SERVES 4

1 tablespoon olive oil

2 red peppers, deseeded, cored and diced

1 red onion, diced

3 teaspoons harissa paste

1 tablespoon sun-dried tomato purée

1 teaspoon caraway seeds

1 teaspoon ground cumin

500 g (1 lb) passata

500 ml (17 fl oz) vegetable stock

400 g (13 oz) can chickpeas, rinsed and drained

salt and pepper

TO SERVE

chilli or olive oil

toasted cumin seeds (see page 37), (optional)

chopped flat leaf parsley

crusty white bread

○ Heat the oil in the soup maker using the sauté function. Add the red peppers and onion and sauté for 7–8 minutes until softened, stirring frequently with a wooden spatula. Stir in the harissa, tomato purée, caraway seeds and cumin and cook, stirring, for another 1–2 minutes.

○ Pour in the passata and stock, then add the chickpeas and season well. Cook on the Chunky setting.

○ Serve the soup in warm bowls, drizzled with a little chilli or olive oil and sprinkled with toasted cumin seeds, chopped parsley and crusty white bread on the side.

SERVES 4

3 corn cobs

1 tablespoon Shaoxing wine

1 tablespoon soy sauce

2 teaspoons peeled and finely chopped fresh root ginger

1.2 litres (2 pints) chicken stock

2 teaspoons cornflour

1 egg, beaten

200 g (7 oz) white crab meat

salt and pepper

2 spring onions, chopped, to garnish

CHINESE CRAB AND SWEETCORN

○ Using a sharp knife, cut the kernels from the corn cobs. Place the kernels, Shaoxing wine, soy sauce, ginger and 1 litre (1¾ pints) of the stock in the soup maker, then cook on the Chunky setting for 10 minutes.

○ Mix the cornflour with the remaining stock, then pour into the soup maker. Continue to cook on Chunky.

○ When the soup maker signals the soup is cooked, immediately remove the lid and, stirring the soup with a large spoon, slowly pour in the egg in one long stream to create silky strands through the soup. Gently stir in the crab meat.

○ Season the soup to taste, the serve in warm bowls, sprinkled with the spring onions.

SERVES 6

2 tablespoons extra virgin olive oil

1 onion, diced

3 garlic cloves, crushed

1 tablespoon finely chopped rosemary

2 x 400 g (13 oz) cans chopped tomatoes

600 ml (1 pint) vegetable stock

400 g (13 oz) can borlotti beans, rinsed and drained

125 g (4 oz) small dried pasta shapes

salt and pepper

grated Parmesan cheese, to serve

FOR THE BASIL OIL (OPTIONAL)

25 g (1 oz) basil leaves

150 ml (¼ pint) extra virgin olive oil

PASTA AND BEAN WITH BASIL OIL

○ Heat the oil in the soup maker using the sauté function. Add the onion, garlic and rosemary and sauté for 5 minutes until the onion is softened, stirring frequently with a wooden spatula.

○ Stir in the tomatoes, stock and beans. Cook on the Chunky setting for 10 minutes. Add the pasta and continue to cook on Chunky.

○ Meanwhile, make the basil oil, if using. Plunge the basil leaves into a saucepan of boiling water for 30 seconds. Drain the basil and refresh under cold running water, then dry thoroughly with kitchen paper. Place the oil and basil leaves in a blender and blend until very smooth.

○ Serve the soup in warm bowls, drizzled with a little of the basil oil, if liked, and sprinkled with some Parmesan.

CHICKEN, CHILLI AND ROSEMARY

SERVES 4

1 tablespoon olive oil

1 onion, diced

2 garlic cloves, crushed

500 g (1 lb) potatoes, peeled and diced

1 litre (1¾ pints) chicken stock

1 red chilli, deseeded and finely chopped, plus extra to garnish

2 tablespoons finely chopped rosemary

1 cooked chicken breast, shredded

salt and pepper

TO SERVE

finely chopped chives

1–2 tablespoons chilli oil

○ Heat the olive oil in the soup maker using the sauté function. Add the onion and garlic and sauté for 3–4 minutes, stirring frequently with a wooden spatula. Add the potatoes and cook for another 2 minutes, stirring to coat in the onion and garlic.

○ Add the stock, chilli and rosemary and season with salt and pepper. Cook on the Smooth setting.

○ Stir the shredded chicken into the soup, then serve in warm bowls, garnished with the chopped chilli and chives and drizzled with the chilli oil.

SERVES 4–6

1 tablespoon sunflower oil

1 onion, diced

2 carrots, diced

500 g (1 lb) tomatoes, skinned, if liked (see page70), and roughly diced

½ teaspoon piri piri seasoning or dried chilli flakes

100 g (3½ oz) roasted salted peanuts, ground to a fine powder in a spice mill or blender, plus extra peanuts, roughly chopped, to garnish

1 litre (1¾ pints) fish or vegetable stock

salt and pepper

dried chilli flakes, to garnish

FOR THE FOO FOO

750 g (1½ lb) yams or potatoes, peeled and diced

3 tablespoons milk

GHANAIAN GROUNDNUT

○ Heat the oil in the soup maker using the sauté function. Add the onion and carrots and sauté for 5 minutes, stirring frequently with a wooden spatula. Stir in the tomatoes and piri piri or chilli flakes and cook for another 1–2 minutes.

○ Stir in the ground peanuts, then pour in the stock and cook on the Chunky setting.

○ Meanwhile, make the foo foo. Cook the yams or potatoes in a saucepan of boiling water for 20 minutes until tender. Drain, then mash with the milk and season to taste. Shape into balls.

○ Turn the soup maker off and on again to activate the blender function, if your machine requires, and pulse a few times to give the soup a thicker consistency.

○ Season the soup to taste, then pour into warm bowls and sprinkle with the chilli flakes and chopped peanuts. Serve the foo foo separately, for dunking into the hot soup.

SERVES 4

2 tablespoons olive oil

1 onion, diced

1 garlic clove, finely chopped

1 teaspoon ground cumin

1 teaspoon ground coriander

pinch of dried chilli flakes

2 small celeriac, peeled and finely diced

2 potatoes, peeled and finely diced

1 litre (1¾ pints) vegetable stock

25 g (1 oz) fresh coriander, chopped

TO SERVE

4 tablespoons crème fraîche

toasted cumin seeds (see page 37)

SPICED POTATO, CORIANDER AND CELERIAC

O Heat the oil in the soup maker using the sauté function. Add the onion and garlic and sauté for 3–4 minutes, stirring frequently with a wooden spatula. Add the ground cumin, ground coriander and chilli flakes and cook, stirring, for another minute.

O Add the celeriac and potatoes, then pour in the stock. Cook on the Smooth setting for 10 minutes. Add the chopped coriander and continue to cook on Smooth.

O Serve the soup in warm bowls, topped with dollops of crème fraîche and sprinkled with toasted cumin seeds.

SERVES 4

2 tablespoons olive oil

1 onion, diced

3 garlic cloves, crushed

1 teaspoon chipotle peppers in adobo sauce, chopped, or Tabasco sauce

2 teaspoons sugar

400 g (13 oz) can chopped tomatoes

1 litre (1¾ pints) chicken stock

salt and pepper

TO SERVE

2 cooked chicken breasts, torn into strips

1 avocado, peeled, stoned and cubed

handful of tortilla chips, crushed

4 tablespoons soured cream

handful of coriander leaves, chopped

SPICY CHICKEN AND TORTILLA

○ Heat the oil in the soup maker using the sauté function. Add the onion and sauté for 5 minutes until softened, stirring frequently with a wooden spatula. Stir in the garlic, chipotle or Tabasco sauce and sugar.

○ Pour in the tomatoes and stock, then cook on the Smooth setting.

○ Season the soup to taste, then pour into warm bowls. Top with the chicken, avocado and tortilla chips. Serve drizzled with the soured cream and sprinkled with the chopped coriander.

SERVES 4

2 tablespoons vegetable oil

1 red onion, diced

1 celery stick, diced

2.5 cm (1 inch) piece of fresh root ginger, peeled and diced

1 tablespoon jerk seasoning

1 kg (2 lb) sweet potatoes (or use a mixture of sweet potato and butternut squash), peeled and diced

1.2 litres (2 pints) chicken stock

2 tablespoons lime juice

250 g (8 oz) cooked chicken, shredded

salt and pepper

thinly sliced spring onions, to garnish

JERK CHICKEN AND SWEET POTATO

○ Heat the oil in the soup maker using the sauté function. Add the onion, celery and ginger and sauté for 4–5 minutes until beginning to soften, stirring frequently with a wooden spatula. Add the jerk seasoning and the sweet potatoes and cook, stirring, for another minute.

○ Pour in the stock, then cook on the Smooth setting.

○ Add the lime juice to the soup and season to taste.

○ Pour into warm bowls and top each with a handful of the shredded chicken. Serve sprinkled with spring onions.

MUSHROOM AND THYME WITH GOATS' CHEESE CROUTES

SERVES 4

3 tablespoons olive oil

1 onion, diced

500 g (1 lb) chestnut mushrooms, roughly diced

2 tablespoons thyme leaves, plus extra to garnish

600 ml (1 pint) chicken or vegetable stock

2 tablespoons Dijon mustard

200 ml (7 fl oz) crème fraîche

salt and pepper

FOR THE GOATS' CHEESE CROUTES

8 thin slices of small French baguette

1 teaspoon Dijon mustard

8 thin slices of rinded goats' cheese

○ Heat the oil in the soup maker using the sauté function. Add the onion and sauté for 3 minutes, stirring frequently with a wooden spatula. Add the mushrooms and thyme leaves and cook for 5 minutes until the mushrooms have softened, stirring occasionally.

○ Pour in the stock and add the mustard, then cook on the Smooth setting for 10 minutes. Add the crème fraîche, season well and continue to cook on Smooth.

○ Meanwhile, make the croutes. Toast the baguette slices under a preheated grill, then thinly spread with the mustard. Top with the goats' cheese slices and cook under the grill for 1–2 minutes until the cheese is just beginning to brown in places.

○ Serve the soup in warm bowls, topped with the croutes and garnished with extra thyme leaves.

INDEX

GLOSSARY

UK	US	UK	US
aubergine	eggplant	deseeded	seeded
back bacon rashers	Canadian bacon slices	double cream	heavy cream
baking paper	parchment paper	dried chilli flakes	red pepper flakes
streaky bacon rashers	lean bacon slices	flaked almonds	sliced almonds
beetroot	beet	grill	broiler/broil
black beans	turtle beans	haricot beans	navy beans
black-eyed beans	black-eye peas	jug	pitcher
borlotti beans	cranberry beans	kitchen paper	paper towels
broad beans	fava beans	mangetout	snow peas
butter beans	lima beans	natural yogurt	plain yogurt
caster sugar	super-fine or granulated sugar	passata	sieved tomatoes
		plain flour	all-purpose flour
celeriac	celery root	red/green pepper	red/green bell pepper
chestnut mushrooms	cremini mushrooms	rocket leaves	arugula
chopped tomatoes (canned)	diced/crushed tomatoes (canned)	semi-skimmed milk	reduced fat milk
		single cream	light cream
coriander leaves	cilantro leaves	spring onions	scallions
cornflour	cornstarch	sultanas	golden raisins
courgette	zucchini	tomato purée	tomato paste

ACKNOWLEDGEMENTS

PICTURE CREDITS

All photographs are by William Shaw for Octopus Publishing, with the exception of the following: Adrian Lawrence 59, 101, 108; Ian Wallace 13, 39, 115; Lis Parsons 3, 15, 41, 43, 48, 49, 67, 91, 96, 111, 128; Sean Myers 44; Simon Smith 48; Stephen Conroy 14, 16, 23, 36, 40, 51, 60, 61, 85, 88, 92, 93, 109, 123; Wil Heap 17, 19, 20, 21, 87, 107, 113, 117, 119, 121; William Lingwood 24; William Reavell 47, 81, 83, 110.

Recipe Development: Joy Skipper
Editorial Director: Eleanor Maxfield
Commissioned by: Cara Armstrong
Copy Editor: Jo Murray
Designer: Geoff Fennell
Picture Research Manager: Giulia Hetherington
Production Manager: Caroline Alberti